THE GRADUATE STUDENTS' GUIDE TO THESES AND DISSERTATIONS

A Practical Manual for Writing and Research

George R. Allen

The Graduate
Students'
Guide to
Theses and
Dissertations

*A Practical
Manual
for Writing
and
Research*

Jossey-Bass Publishers
San Francisco • Washington • London • 1979

THE GRADUATE STUDENTS' GUIDE TO THESES AND DISSERTATIONS
A Practical Manual for Writing and Research
   by George R. Allen

Copyright © 1973 by: Jossey-Bass, Inc., Publishers
                     433 California Street
                     San Francisco, California 94104

                     and

                     Jossey-Bass Limited
                     28 Banner Street
                     London EC1Y 8QE

Library of Congress Catalogue Card Number LC 73-3774

International Standard Book Number ISBN 0-87589-182-9

Manufactured in the United States of America

JACKET DESIGN BY WILLI BAUM

FIRST EDITION
      First printing: September 1973
      Second printing: March 1974
      Third printing: February 1975
      Fourth printing: December 1976
      Fifth printing: October 1979

Code 7324

Preface

The objective of *The Graduate Students' Guide to Theses and Dissertations* is to assist faculty members and students in completing high-quality theses and dissertations without wasting time and effort. Although good research does, of course, require time and effort, many factors that extend time do not increase the quality of the final report or teach the student anything worthwhile about academic research. Proper planning before the research is started can significantly reduce the time required to produce high-quality work. In fact, the student who uses the material and suggestions in this book from the beginning of his doctoral program should be able to complete his dissertation within one academic year after his comprehensives are completed.

The Graduate Students' Guide to Theses and Dissertations presents an integrated and comprehensive overview of the dissertation and thesis process, so that the graduate student can visualize this research activity from beginning to end. Often the researcher is concerned only with the step of immediate importance to him and gives little thought to the steps that remain. Thus, pending problems are not foreseen, and formidable obstacles emerge. But, by taking an organized and systematic approach to the whole process, the researcher can anticipate and avoid or minimize many of the problems.

To highlight the various problems and issues in the research process, I have used a question-and-answer format. Questions are asked and answered as briefly and succinctly as possible, and most of the suggestions would require very little time for a graduate student to implement. Each chapter, then, contains commonly asked questions, with appropriate answers, concerning the steps involved in academic research. Many of these questions are controversial, and a wide range of answers could be given. The particular answers given here represent my own opinions; but these opinions have been discussed with educators and students throughout the country. To minimize the extent of possible disagreement, a generalized answer is given; and at all times the student is referred to his research committee for definitive answers to critical questions.

Seven steps in the research process are outlined: selecting a research topic, getting a research committee, preparing a research proposal, collecting data, analyzing data, writing the final report, and defending the research effort. Since these steps are similar for most areas of academic research, the material presented should have general applicability. The Bibliography contains an extensive list of selected publications covering a wide range of academic disciplines.

Each chapter has three components: an introduction stating the purpose and coverage of the chapter and relating that step to the steps preceding and following it; a series of questions and answers about that step in the research process; a list of questions about the interests of the researcher and the philosophy and procedures at the school where the research is being conducted. These questions should help the student to avoid avoidable mistakes, mistakes that do not contribute to the learning process relating to academic research.

The Graduate Students' Guide to Theses and Dissertations

Preface

does not address certain aspects of academic research. It does not
dwell at length upon format and methodology, already adequately
covered in the literature. It does not advocate any particular technique for conducting research. It does not try to underestimate the
difficulties of completing theses or dissertations. Most important, it
does not try to preempt the judgment of the faculty members who
are working with students. An effort is made to get the student
thinking about the important aspects of academic research and to
eliminate the need for the research chairman and committee to
answer routine questions over and over again for different students.
The student is given some answers, advised to seek many answers for
himself, and recommended to his research committee only for the
important questions and always with specific questions in mind.

Finally, the book does not assume that all theses and dissertations can or should be written in precisely the same fashion. It does
not attempt to produce stereotyped, sterile, mass-produced pieces of
research that could drain the lifeblood from academic research.
There is ample opportunity for creative writing and creative thinking in the research process. However, research is research, and the
scientific method of collecting and analyzing data does not differ
much with the topic being researched. Use of the basic guidelines
presented here should sharpen the focus of the research, eliminate
much wasted time and effort, and facilitate the orderly and efficient
completing of dissertation writing. Ultimately, this should mean that
more doctoral candidates will receive their degrees, doctoral com-
mittees will be more efficiently utilized, and the trauma often
associated with the final stages of doctoral programs will be
diminished.

I wish to thank the students at Arizona State University,
George Washington University, the University of Oklahoma, and
The American University for their assistance in helping me formulate the material in this book. Their critical comments and suggestions, offered at various seminars, were most helpful. My special
thanks go to Daniel Roman and William Sproull, who provided
much helpful material; to J. D. Brown, George Humphries, Benja-

Preface

min Sands, Robert Blumel, William Halal, Jerome Hanus, Conway Lackman, Paul Arvis, Carlyle Hughes, Justin Voss, James Sharf, Art Meiners, and Daniel Roman, who reviewed the manuscript; and to Eleanor Loewenthal, Kathy Goetz, Lillian Strickland and Sherri Di Carlo, who typed the drafts and the final manuscript. Keith Davis taught me much of what I know about academic research when he served as my research advisor at Arizona State University. I am deeply indebted to him.

Arlington, Virginia
February 1973

GEORGE R. ALLEN

Contents

THE GRADUATE STUDENTS'
GUIDE TO THESES
AND DISSERTATIONS

A Practical Manual for
Writing and Research

ONE

Academic Research

This chapter does not focus on any specific step in the research process. Instead, some commonly asked general questions are answered here in order to provide a basis for the chapters to follow. In the other chapters attention is focused upon the step being developed.

At the end of this chapter is a list of questions directed toward the school that the student is attending.

What is the purpose of a doctoral dissertation?

A dissertation is an exercise in research. It is the process of learning how to conduct research, so that the student may continue to uncover or produce knowledge after his graduate school days are behind him. In fact, the entire doctoral program is often thought to be one of *developing and demonstrating competency in research.* Successful completion of a dissertation should demonstrate to the research committee that the candidate is capable of pursuing independent research under the proper guidance of his committee. Then he should be capable of independently conducting research and, later, of directing such efforts on the part of other students, should he choose an academic career.

The dissertation is a formal written work, a scholarly document. It should be conducted on an advanced level, and the candidate should demonstrate that he is able to produce and interpret meaningful results.

A dissertation is supposed to be a "Contribution to Knowledge." What is a contribution to knowledge?

What represents a contribution to one faculty member may not be considered as such by another faculty member. Therefore, you should discuss your potential topic with the person who might be acting as director of your research to get his interpretations of the relative contribution of the topic. He might suggest that a contribution represents some advancement in the state of the art; a breakthrough in some theory; formulation of a new theory; refutation of an existing theory; addition to an existing theory; new insights into human, physical, or natural sciences; establishing of new relationships; or a creative accomplishment.

Remember, however, that the more ambitious your aims are in the dissertation, the more difficulty you can expect and the longer it will take you to complete the research. And, more important, the more time you take, the less your chances of ever completing the work, for reasons largely *beyond your control.* (These reasons are discussed elsewhere.)

I would not ask you to reduce your ambitions or to intentionally minimize the contribution you wish to make. Set goals as high as you wish, as long as you realize the potential impact your decision will have on your ever completing the dissertation. The guidelines offered in this book are designed to produce significant contributions to knowledge. But you must strike a balance between the possibility of making a contribution of significant importance and the probability of *ever* completing your degree requirements.

This book assumes that faculty members and students want to perform a scholarly job of research, one that they can be proud of, in a reasonable length of time. So carve out a manageable area for the dissertation and demonstrate to your committee that you are capable of conducting research. After you have successfully defended the dissertation, you will have plenty of time to develop your reputation as a researcher.

Do different fields (such as the social sciences and the physical sciences) have different requirements for an acceptable dissertation or thesis?

Yes. There are differences, for instance, in the techniques of data collection and analysis, in the precision of measurement, in the time reference of topics (past, present, or future), in the degree of quantification expected or possible, and in the expected length of the paper. Despite these differences, however, there is a great deal of similarity in the *process* of academic research, which is the focus of this book.

Why should I worry about the dissertation process now, since my comprehensives are about two years away?

This book is of more value to the beginning doctoral student than to the student who has already passed his comprehensives and is preparing to write his dissertation. Many of the suggestions made here cannot be used by the person who has completed everything except the dissertation.

The best time to begin your preparations for writing a dissertation or thesis is when you start your program of study. The poorest time to start is after you have completed your comprehensives. Why?

First, there will be a certain amount of time wasted in the

search for an acceptable topic. You can overlap this wasted time with the successful completion of other parts of your program.

Second, the ability to conduct research can be developed while you are completing your course requirements; when the courses are completed, no time is left for such experimentation.

Third, many of the suggestions contained in this book pertain to overall completion of the doctoral or master's program and are of more value if you have ample time to utilize the hints and suggestions.

Can I afford to waste any of my scarce time working on the dissertation when I first have to complete my courses and the comprehensives?

The dissertation is the last hurdle in the doctoral program, as the thesis is often the last hurdle in the master's program. If the earlier parts of the graduate program are not completed successfully, there will be no thesis or dissertation to prepare. Here is where you must make a personal assessment of your ability to do more than one thing at a time. If you can handle the course work and do preliminary work on the dissertation, then you are managing your time well. Since many of the suggestions in this book require almost no time to implement, every doctoral student should be able to overlap the earlier parts of his program with preliminary work on the dissertation.

If your are not confident of your ability to implement some of these suggestions in the early part of your program, then concentrate on getting a solid footing in your program before earnestly starting on the preliminary dissertation work. If you read this book in your first semester of the doctoral program, you should find yourself using the suggestions on term papers and other research projects. This will not only help you in your program, but indirectly it will start you on your dissertation or thesis with almost no extra effort.

4

Since I am going to make a large investment in time on the dissertation, why not write a paper that can be published?

Nothing in this book should be interpreted to suggest that you write a dissertation and place it on a shelf, never to be used again. If you follow the suggestions that are offered, you should have a research report that can be published after the defense. At this point, however, you will do well to concentrate on getting the dissertation completed and defended and not become distracted with thoughts of later publications. These will take care of themselves. If you divert your attention to potential publications while preparing your dissertation, you may end up with a publication and no dissertation. Moreover, since many schools require that the research results *not* appear in published form until after the dissertation has been successfully defended, premature publication may even *jeopardize* your dissertation.

Your job search may, of course, be more successful if you have a publication or two in addition to the dissertation. If you can accomplish both, give it a try. To repeat, anything that diverts your time and efforts away from the dissertation has a risk asssociated with it. Can you afford the risk?

How much time should it take to complete a dissertation?

The time will vary with the individual, the school, the topic, and a great many other factors. In general, however, a high-quality dissertation can be started and completed within one academic year—if you have that as your primary objective for the year and can remain at the university and devote almost all your efforts to the project. If you leave the university, then the minimum time period should be two years, and three is a more realistic expectation.

To minimize your time requirements, which is a major objective of this book, stay at or near the university until you have defended your dissertation. If that is impossible, leave only after

5

you have an approved topic, the data collected, and the first draft in your committee's hands.

Why should I be in a hurry to complete my research?

The more time you spend on your research, the less your chances are of ever completing; and most of the factors working against you are completely out of your control. Here are some of those factors:

Faculty members are mobile. They change positions, they take sabbaticals, they go away for the summer, they retire. What happens when the chairman of your committee leaves the university? At some schools the faculty member is *allowed,* but not required, to continue as your advisor. At other schools the faculty member would *not be allowed* to remain as your chairman. What if no other person on the faculty is willing to accept your topic? You may have to start over again with a new topic. It happens all too often. How much control do you have over the mobility of the members of your research committee?

A hot topic will cool down with the passage of time. The longer you spend on your topic, the cooler your topic will become. The more you compress the time, the more you are apt to capitalize on the heat of the topic. Furthermore, as time is extended, you and members of your committee may lose interest in the subject. Some doctoral students eventually lose all interest and give up, never completing their research and never getting their degree.

Several other scholars may be working in the same area and may produce results that could invalidate your entire work. As a result, you could be forced to abandon the topic and select a new one—starting the process of research from the beginning.

If you are working in an area that is undergoing rapid changes, with new research emerging each day, you may be forced to continue your literature search for an extended period of time. You may even have to make major revisions in parts of the final paper that you had considered finished. Or the process of rapid change may force you to make a major effort in preparation for the final defense.

Finally, most people find it hard to begin (let alone complete) serious writing after an extended period of procrastination or inactivity. As the time frame expands, it becomes very difficult to muster up enough initiative to complete the final writing.

I have a great job offer that I will lose if I don't accept it now. What difference will it make if I complete the dissertation while I am working at my job?

Stay at the university until you have completed your dissertation. If you leave the university after you have completed your comprehensives but before you have finished the dissertation, your chances of ever completing your dissertation probably will drop to less than 50–50. All factors work against you when you leave the university. Let's explore some of the reasons for staying.

First, your research committeee chairman, usually the key man in your research, is readily available when you are at the university. He can be consulted on many of the problems that will arise as your work progresses. If you leave the university, you must rely upon the mails to contact the chairman, introducing an enormous delay in correspondence, even under ideal delivery schedules. A small problem that might be solved in minutes if you were at the university might take a month when handled by remote correspondence.

Your chairman is probably up to date on the area in which you are writing. If you are available and in mind, he may bring to your attention items that should be included in your research. If you are not there, these items may slip his mind, and you may find out about them when you have to make major revisions in your report.

Furthermore, as mentioned, during the longer time it will take you to complete your dissertation away from the university, your chairman or some key member of your research committee

7

may leave the university and become unavailable to you even by mail.

When you leave the university without having the dissertation finished, it should take you two or three years to complete it—*if you ever do*. Thus, if you accept the assumption that a dissertation can be written in one academic year by staying at the university and devoting large segments of time to it, leaving the university costs you at least two years of time and significantly raises the odds *against* your ever completing. Could the rewards be worth the risk?

To repeat, stay at the university until you complete the dissertation—or at least until you have the first draft completed. You can ignore most of the advice in this book, and accept this one suggestion, and significantly speed up your dissertation process.

Are there any particular problems that I might encounter in trying to get financial assistance (a grant or other funding) for my research?

Two major problems come to mind.

First, a proposal is usually required for a grant or funding. This proposal will require time and effort on your part, and then it must go through an approval process. The time that you must spend in preparing the proposal, and in waiting for the reply, can easily extend into months or up to a year or more. In the meantime, you will feel uncomfortable proceeding with the project if the funding is required to complete the work.

Second, you may become entangled in an attempt to serve two masters. In trying to meet the requirements of the funding agency or organization, and in trying to meet the academic requirements of the school, you might be unable to reach a common ground. Even if you do, you may have to spend a lot of time in the process.

There are other problems. For instance, you may become tempted to overlook the criteria for a good dissertation or thesis topic in order to qualify for a grant. Or your work may be "stretched" by both the school and the funding agency until it loses all semblance of what you intended to do. Why not discuss this problem with your chairman? Perhaps a scholarship, assistantship, or fellowship would be available as a more realistic alternative to a grant.

Can you suggest some ways that I could reduce the cost of my research?

1. Check all available financial sources at the school. There are often small grants that require no obligation on the part of the researcher.

2. Select a topic where the data collection involves little or no travel outside your immediate area.

3. Do as much preliminary planning on your research work as you can. This will speed up the process, thus reducing your costs.

4. Try to get the free use of such facilities as a typewriter, supplies and papers, reproducing equipment, clerical or typing assistance, and computer time if required.

5. If you are working with a group or an organization, see whether they will give you any assistance; in return you can give them a copy of your report or a summary of your findings.

6. Don't spend an inordinate amount of time trying to find a topic that will be completely financed, unless you think that the odds are heavily in your favor. You might waste more time trying to get the funds than you would need to do the entire research project.

HERE ARE A FEW QUESTIONS ABOUT THE GENERAL PROCESS OF ACADEMIC RESEARCH. THEY ARE SPECIFICALLY RELATED TO YOUR SCHOOL AND ARE PRESENTED HERE TO GUIDE YOUR THINKING IN YOUR RESEARCH EFFORT.

1. What is the general definition of a thesis or dissertation at your school?

2. What material related to the thesis or dissertation process is available at your school?

3. Are there policies and guidelines for research?

4. What is the average length of time that it takes for completing a thesis or dissertation?

5. Does the school encourage or discourage students to remain at the school after the doctoral comprehensives are successfully passed? Are funds available for this purpose?

6. How do members of the faculty at your school define a "contribution to knowledge"?

7. What members of the faculty would you most like to work with on your research? What are their thoughts on the thesis and the dissertation process?

8. When are doctoral students or master's students permitted to begin the official research effort? Must doctoral students wait until the comprehensives are completed before submitting the dissertation proposal?

9. What is the attitude of the faculty toward the swift completion of the research effort? Do they equate speed (or delay) with quality?

10. What is your purpose for writing the dissertation or thesis? What do you hope to accomplish with your research effort?

TWO

Selecting the Research Topic

The serious graduate student should have little difficulty in finding a suitable thesis or dissertation topic. In fact, his main problem should be how to select—from the number of potential topics he has uncovered—the one best suited to his interests. This chapter attempts to make the task of selecting a research topic less arduous and presents several sources of research topics.

Since no one can decide for you what specific topic to research, the material here is presented in such a fashion that you should be able to develop a set of criteria for evaluating potential topics. If you know the criteria by which a potential topic can be evaluated, and where to look for potential topics, you are well on the way toward selecting a suitable topic.

The chapter also contains (on the pages immediately preceding the final list of questions) a checklist of questions which could constitute the beginning of your *personalized* set of criteria for evaluating research topics. You may wish to review this checklist prior to reading the chapter (pages 22–26).

At the end of the chapter there is a list of questions that should be helpful in determining what additional information you need about topics at your school or university.

What are the characteristics of a potential topic?

The potential topic should be of current or future interest in your field of study—a topic that is being discussed or debated in the leading journals and by the leaders in the field. Your own interest in the topic should be strong enough to be sustained throughout the time you are conducting the research.

The potential topic should be narrow and specific instead of broad and nebulous. Many doctoral candidates mistakenly select a topic far too broad and indefinite to be thoroughly researched and written. Few students select topics that are too narrow. Reduce the scope of your potential topic until the area of study is manageable. The mark of an effective researcher (which is what you are trying to become) is an ability to clearly delineate and isolate the problem area for investigation.

In addition, the topic should be of interest to the faculty members with whom you hope to be working and should be accessible to research; that is, it should have readily obtainable data and should lend itself to a data-collection technique that can be pretested and that will produce usable data.

Finally, you should be able to visualize the potential topic from data collection to written report—to anticipate all the major problems you will encounter, along with the approaches you will use to minimize or eliminate these problems.

Determining whether a topic has potential for scholarly research is perhaps the biggest problem in the dissertation and thesis process. Such an evaluation can be made only after the researcher has developed criteria for selecting a topic. These criteria are seldom reduced to writing, and the researcher blindly searches for means to evaluate the topic. For a suggested statement of criteria, see the Checklist for Evaluating Potential Research Topics at the end of this chapter (pages 22–26).

How interested should I be in the dissertation topic?

The more intense your interest, the less likely you will be to give up on the topic if you encounter time or other difficulties. Since interest must be sustained for a minimum of a few months to a few years, take care to uncover a topic that has been of interest to you and is likely to remain of interest for the near future.

One word of caution is needed, however. Do not become too wedded to an area of interest that does not meet the other criteria for an effective dissertation topic. Don't try to warp an area that you like, but that contains too many unknowns, into a dissertation topic. Save that project for your first major writing effort *after* you complete the dissertation. Look critically, harshly, objectively, and rationally at your potential topics. It is too easy to brush aside pending problems in an area of intense interest and to let emotions control. Resist this temptation to overlook problems or to minimize them. You may regret it later, and may jeopardize your chances of completing your dissertation.

Some members of the faculty think that I have a potential topic for a dissertation; others think it has no potential whatsoever. Why such a wide divergence of viewpoints in the same faculty?

Circulate any topic widely enough and you will find a full range of opinions about it. Some will think it is excellent, while others will think it has no potential whatsoever. This diversity of opinion can probably be found on almost any faculty. Thus, expect to encounter a wide range of opinions. One possible reason is that few faculties decide (and put this decision in writing) exactly what a dissertation is or should be. The definition exists in the mind of each faculty member, reflecting his current interests, biases, expertise, experiences. There probably cannot be a precise, universal standard for what is acceptable research at the master's or doctoral level. Consequently, there must be latitude in the definition of dissertation topics, and only the research committee members should have to certify that a topic has potential for it to be accepted.

How strongly should I try to sell the merits of my topic?

If you must strenuously sell your research committee on the merits of your topic, you might be starting an uphill battle that is not worth the fight. If the committee can be convinced (really convinced) of the merits of the topic without excessive selling on your part, then the topic may be right for you.

Once a committee has rejected a topic, after repeated efforts on your part to sell its merits, there is little reason for pursuing the topic. A negative attitude might become locked in, and the committee members may feel committed to their negative decision. Drop such a topic.

Even if you do convince the committee, you may be asking for problems later. The feeling of "I told you that the topic was no good" may persist, and you may have to abandon the topic after a considerable loss of time.

Since there are many possible research topics, your difficulty should be one of selecting from among many that may be suitable. The right topic will be recognized after sufficient preliminary investigation. Don't spend inordinate time on a lost cause.

When should I start looking for a dissertation topic?

You should start looking for a topic at the very beginning of your doctoral program—or even sooner. You cannot begin too soon. You won't, of course, start writing the thesis or dissertation in your

14

first semester, and you probably won't begin looking for a research committee when you enter your first class. But you can at least start to think constructively about the requirement for research. If you begin looking for a topic after the comprehensives are completed, you will have lost all the opportunities to overlap your search with your course work and other parts of your graduate program.

My school has a rule that we are not permitted even to talk about our research projects before the comprehensives are completed, let alone begin any part of the process. What do I do?

The basis of the rule is probably to take first things first and to do one task at a time. But such a rule seems inconsistent with the way many people look at a doctoral program of study. Many people feel that the entire program builds toward the dissertation—that the purpose of a doctoral program is to develop and demonstrate research competence; so how could it be of any advantage to wait until the comprehensives are completed before looking for research topics and developing research competence? Surely no school can believe that you must not start learning about research until after you have completed all courses and the comprehensives.

If your school has the rule, and won't be changing it soon enough to benefit you, you may still be able to begin the process. You can look for possible topics, test them with term papers, sharpen your skills of research, attend oral defenses, work with professors who are interested in ideas you have for research, and do a great many tasks that may lead you into the path of a proper topic for research. You can reserve the *formal* start on your dissertation topic selection until the time authorized by your school. In other words, do all that you can in an informal manner; but do not broadcast your progress. Abide by the rules of your school. In the meantime, try to encourage a change of this rule.

I am preparing for the comprehensives. Why should I be bothered with looking for dissertation topics?

A doctoral student should not find himself looking for a dissertation topic at the comprehensive stage of his program. He should have been involved in the selection process and have developed and tested his research skills long before this time. Also, if he has formulated criteria for an acceptable topic as recommended, then he will see many potential topics in his review for the comprehensives. He need only jot these down for later reference and continue preparation for his comprehensives. He need not spend any time assessing or evaluating the topics, merely *capturing the potential idea for later evaluation.*

I just reviewed several dissertations that were approved at my school and was surprised. They did not seem like dissertations to me. How could they have been approved and defended?

What has happened to you is a common occurrence in schools across the country. Many doctoral students have either no idea of what a dissertation is or a very high opinion of what it should be. That is, doctoral students often overestimate the requirements for a dissertation and are therefore surprised when they review dissertations that have been successfully defended at their school.

You should be encouraged by your experience. As a matter of fact, this comment is often made: "If that is all that is required for a dissertation, then I should have no trouble doing that kind of research." Or "If he or she can write a dissertation, then I certainly can." So be encouraged when you review dissertations. You *can* conduct such research, and you should feel that you are capable of producing a high-quality research project.

What are the advantages and disadvantages of using term papers as springboards to theses or dissertations?

On the advantage side, term papers offer a chance to explore a topic and review the literature related to the subject. The student may also have a chance to utilize some of his statistical knowledge in the paper. In addition, the simple process of preparing the written paper could contribute to easing the thesis or dissertation burden. Writing several increasingly large term papers may gear the student for the requirement to write a paper of one hundred to three hundred pages. Thus, if the term paper is conducted as a "mini-research" effort, the practical experience of preparing the paper can make a positive contribution to the writing of a thesis or dissertation.

On the disadvantage side, the student may feel that he has invested so much time in this topic that he can't even consider anything else for the thesis or dissertation. He may become "locked in" to a particular topic and mistakenly assume that all his time and effort have been wasted if he must choose another topic.

Avoid the tendency to become enamored with a topic that does not have true potential for a thesis or dissertation. Do not try to warp a topic that made a good term paper into a thesis or dissertation when the evidence strongly suggests that another topic is needed. Many professors will approve a topic for a course term paper that they would *never consider* for a thesis or dissertation. The scholarly effort required for a thesis or dissertation is far in excess of that required for a term paper. Thus, the topics amenable to term papers may be vastly different from those required for the thesis or dissertation.

If the term paper topic does not appear to be suitable for a thesis or dissertation, drop it and try to find a suitable topic for your research. Consider the time you spent in the term paper as valuable, since it probably assisted in the development of your skill in doing research and in the preparation of the required final written document.

Consider this question: "Could you finish your thesis or dissertation in a shorter time and with less problems if you switch to a new topic?" If you can increase your chances of completing your research requirements by selecting a new topic, then by all means do so. Don't gamble when you have a reasonable alternative.

Thus, term papers can contribute to your development of research skills and may even give you a potential dissertation or

17

thesis topic, but be aware of the dangers of becoming too involved with a topic to clearly evaluate its potential. Evaluate your term paper against the criteria given in this chapter. If it stands up favorably, you may have a potential topic. If it does not fare too well, drop the topic and select a new one.

What are some other possible sources of potential topics?

Normal class work. Often during a class discussion or lecture the professor will say, *"That* would make an excellent thesis or dissertation topic" or *"That* would make a good research topic." The alert graduate student will jot down the professor's suggestion in a file he is accumulating. Later on he will have the chance to evaluate the real potential of the topic, using some of the criteria suggested in this chapter.

If the topic has real appeal, he might arrange a meeting with the professor to get more of his ideas on the topic. Often the topic is related to a burning interest of the professor or to some consulting that he is doing; the fortunate student then might find a good potential topic and a potential research director at the same time.

Keep the back of your notebooks available (or a separate notebook) to jot down suggested topics during your classes. These suggestions may end up as term papers with no dissertation or thesis potential, or they could end up as term papers that later are developed into full-blown research efforts.

Published abstracts. These sources should be investigated by every doctoral student. The library at your school or at a nearby school should have them. Published abstracts indicate the types of studies completed by other graduate students. The mere reading of abstracts from successful graduate research should provide a psychological lift to you. You should also be able to determine the kinds of topics that are being researched at other institutions as well as those at your own school.

The abstracts are usually arranged by year and general topic areas. Check the index to find the classification that most nearly matches your area of interest. However, look also at related areas. They will enlarge your scope of vision and may suggest topics that you might have considered as not within your area of expertise. Also, going outside your narrow classification might suggest approaches and techniques that could be applicable to your research effort.

A long-range consideration also should be kept in mind. At your defense you may be asked what others have written in the general area of your research. The fact that you have checked the published abstracts is in your favor at the defense.

Local organizations or groups. Local organizations or groups (clinics, hospitals, schools, newspapers, businesses, political organizations) sometimes are in need of research on a problem of particular concern to them. Such groups are often sources of good research projects and sometimes have funds available to assist in the research. Often a thesis or dissertation can be written on a problem that is of concern to persons or firms in the area and yet is general enough to be accepted as a scholarly effort that contributes to the knowledge in the field. Contact any of your friends who work in the area in which you will be writing and see whether possible topics can be generated.

A word of caution is in order: Be aware of the inherent difficulty of trying to satisfy the university and an organization or group.

Current journals. As you are reading articles for assignments or for term papers, keep alert for possible thesis or dissertation topics. Again, it might be wise to have a "potential research topics" notebook that you keep with you at all times, or you could reserve the back of each class notebook for possible topics. Then when you are reading any journal, you can jot down possible topics as you come across them.

Current theories. Have there been any new theories developed in your field? Are there serious questions being raised about existing theories that might suggest research possibilities? Suppose that a theory has been developed and tested on one occupational group. You might develop an acceptable research effort to test the *generality* of the theory by applying it to another occupational group. There are large bonuses to be gained if you can replicate an existing theory. The procedures for data collection, data analysis, and methodology are often readily available, thus saving a great deal of time. Or you might *question* the data collection, data analysis, or methodology used, and base your research effort on an attempt to see whether the theory is supported when different methods are used to collect and analyze the data.

Doctoral defenses. Many times the doctoral defense will suggest several topics that are worthy of separate treatment or will prompt an expansion of the scope of one that has already been completed, approved, and defended. (You might even get potential members for your research committee from among those who have served on the research committee for the research just completed.) Attend as many doctoral or thesis defenses as you can. You may be rewarded for your efforts by uncovering several possible research topics. In addition, you will learn something about what happens at a dissertation defense.

Approved theses or dissertations at your school. You are writing your research for a particular school. Wouldn't it be interesting and worthwhile to see what research has been done by others at that school? If your school has a doctoral students' association or a master's students' association, perhaps they will have files of dissertations or the abstracts of these dissertations.

If completed theses or dissertations are available, check the last chapter, under a section often entitled "suggestions for additional research." Good research generates a need for additional exploration. This source may suggest several topics related to the topic you are interested in pursuing.

Student associations. Does your school have a doctoral students' association or a master's students' association? If it does (and it should), you might suggest that an informal meeting be held once a year, or once a semester, to explore possible topics for research. Faculty members might be invited to discuss their ideas of what constitutes an acceptable dissertation topic. Students who have completed or who are completing their research might be invited to dis-

20

cuss other topics that they have uncovered. Find out which students have topics that have been accepted and ask them about other topics that they may have uncovered before they finally decided on one. Students are less reluctant to share information on topics *after* they have an approved one for themselves. Often a student has ideas for topics that are not in his area and is willing to discuss these ideas with others.

In checking the dissertation abstracts to see whether others have written on a topic I am considering, how many years back should I go?

That question must be answered by the potential or existing chairman of your research committee. If research has not been conducted within the previous five years, then sufficient change should have occurred to indicate that your research would be an updated approach.

Of course, the nature of your topic, and the number of current changes in it, would be the determining factors. A more changeable field would tolerate closely spaced research. One that is relatively stable would require research more widely spaced in time. Once you have the approval of the committee chairman as to the time period to search, then you can proceed. You have then effectively excluded work beyond the cutoff point.

CHECKLIST FOR EVALUATING POTENTIAL RESEARCH TOPICS

If you have several potential topics that you are considering, and you would like to narrow the list to those with the most potential, this checklist could be very helpful. Match each of the topics to the list and eliminate (temporarily) topics that produce the most NO answers on those criteria that you feel are important. (You may wish to assign weights to the questions or to resequence them in order of importance to you.) Those receiving the most YES answers could be explored in more depth. This process might save you the time of thoroughly researching each topic in order to make a final selection.

General Questions:

1. Is this topic one that I can narrow in scope to produce a manageable research project?
2. Is this topic of current interest in my field of study?
3. Will this topic make a specific contribution to knowledge, as defined by my research committee or potential chairman?
4. Can I visualize what work I will have to do during the entire research effort, from the proposal to the defense?
5. Can I draft a tentative table of contents for the final report?
6. Is the topic one that will have general applicability; that is, is it broad in its implication and impact?
7. Has this topic received only minimal coverage in the journals and in related academic research? (Has it *not* been researched extensively?)
8. Can I visualize all major problems that I might encounter, and their tentative solutions, at this time?
9. Do I have an interest in this topic now, and can this interest be sustained throughout the length of the research effort?
10. Will the literature search be manageable?
11. Is the topic similar to others that have been approved at this school? (If it is different, will it be acceptable without a great deal of selling of the topic?)
12. Will the topic require minimum financial assistance?
13. Is the financial assistance that would be needed readily available?
14. Is this topic of interest to a potential research committee chairman that I would like to work with?
15. Is this potential committee chairman someone who is respected by the faculty?
16. Would the topic permit me to avoid having as committee chairman someone whom I would like to avoid?
17. Would this topic permit me to get a research committee that I would like to work with?
18. Would the committee that I have in mind for the topic be sold on the topic?
19. Would I have to do a minimum amount of selling the topic?
20. Can I get all members of the research committee to approve the topic (if that is required)?
21. Will the research committee that this topic suggests, or that I would like to have, be available for the entire length of time that I will be conducting the research?

22. Have I checked to see that no potential member of the research committee is going on sabbatical during the time I will be conducting the research?
23. Have I checked to see whether any faculty member who might be on the research committee is going to retire, or take a leave of absence, during the time I will be conducting the research?
24. Is this research the type that I could defend?
25. Is the data that I will need readily available? Am I certain that I will be able to collect the data?
26. Will I have to travel very little to collect the data? Is the data in this immediate area?
27. Will I have almost complete control over the data collection?
28. Will I be able to minimize my bias toward this topic? Is the bias that I have easily controlled?
29. Can I precisely state the purpose, scope, objectives, and limitations of the study?
30. Do I have all the required skills to complete this topic? Are those I lack easily obtained?

If you will be using a research question or hypothesis approach, then you might also use these questions to evaluate potential topics:

1. Can I specifically state my research questions or hypotheses?
2. Do I know the exact manner in which I will test these questions or hypotheses?
3. Am I *uncertain* which of these research questions or hypotheses will be supported or rejected by the research?
4. Can these questions or hypotheses be accepted or rejected on the basis of acceptable logic, statistical tests, or experimentation?
5. Am I proficient in the techniques and methods that will be needed to test the research questions or hypotheses?
6. Can I get a faculty member on the research committee who will be able to assist me in any area where I might be weak?
7. Would my final paper be acceptable to my research committee if my findings do *not* support my questions or hypotheses?
8. Am I certain that I can collect *relevant* data to adequately test each of my research questions or hypotheses?
9. Am I certain that I will be able to control the data-collection process so that my data will be valid and reliable?
10. Am I able to state and test any subsidiary questions?

If you will be using an interview approach to data collection, then you might also use these questions to evaluate potential topics:

1. Is an interview approach appropriate for this type of topic?
2. Do I have the proper qualifications to conduct the types of interviews I will need?
3. Do I know exactly whom I will interview?
4. Do I know exactly how many interviews I should conduct?
5. Will I definitely be able to get the required number of interviews?
6. Do I know precisely what information I will need from each interviewee?
7. Can I formulate the exact questions I will ask each person?
8. Will I be able to reduce my "interviewer's bias" to an acceptable level?
9. Will I be able to elicit the proper responses to properly address my research questions or hypotheses?
10. Is my research committee fully in favor of the interview approach?
11. Could I combine the interview approach with another method for collecting data?
12. If respondent identity is a problem, can I solve the problem?

If you plan to use a questionnaire to collect your data, then you might also use these questions to evaluate potential topics:

1. Does this topic lend itself readily to the use of a questionnaire?
2. Is the use of survey data collected by questionnaires acceptable to potential committee members?
3. Is there an existing questionnaire that has been tested for validity and reliability that I could use for my study? Is this an acceptable procedure to use?
4. Can I draft a tentative questionnaire that will indicate the specific information I will need to complete my research?
5. Will I be able to relate each question on the questionnaire to my research questions or hypotheses?
6. Do I have a convenient method or location for pretesting my questionnaire?
7. Is the questionnaire that I will need one that could be converted to punched cards and analyzed on a computer? (There are several general-purpose computer programs that are able to analyze a wide variety of questionnaires *if* the questionnaires are designed properly.) (See also the questions and answers related to the use of questionnaires in Chapter Five.)

Selecting the Research Topic

If you will be using statistical or mathematical techniques to analyze your data, then you might also use these questions to evaluate the topic:

1. Does this topic lend itself to the use of quantitative analysis?
2. Am I familiar with the specific techniques that will be needed?
3. Are standard tests available; if not, can I modify one of the standard tests?
4. Am I able to state the level of confidence at which I will accept or reject my research questions or hypotheses?
5. Can the data be readily quantified? Will there be a minimum of interpretation required to reduce the data to terms that can be quantified?
6. Will I be able to get a statistician on the committee whom I would like to work with?
7. Are there "canned" programs at the computer center that will be available to do the computations for me?
8. If there are no available programs on the computer, can I still use the computer with a minimum of time and expense? (There is no necessary reason why the computer has to be used, but it is often very helpful with research that uses statistical methods of analysis.)
9. Will the use of quantitative analysis make the defense of the dissertation relatively easy?
10. Can I combine a subjective analysis with the quantitative analysis to produce a more meaningful piece of research?

If you plan to use data that is already published, then you might use these questions to evaluate the potential topic:

1. Is this technique acceptable to all members of my research committee?
2. Is this the best method for collecting data on this topic?
3. Could I (should I) also collect additional data to supplement the published data?
4. Is the data reliable and valid?
5. Do I have the latest edition of the data?
6. Is it unlikely that the data will be revised prior to the completion of my final report and the dissertation defense?
7. Is the data source reliable?
8. Is the data adjusted for seasonal variation (if appropriate)?
9. Are the probable errors in the data within tolerable limits, so that they will present no problems for me?

10. Have I avoided any bias in selecting the data base?
11. If other data bases could have been used, can I justify the selection I have made?
12. Will the data base permit me to adequately address my research question or hypotheses?

If you plan to use testing instruments for your data collection, you might also use these questions to evaluate potential topics:

1. Is the test I plan to use appropriate for my study?
2. Are there other tests that could be used?
3. Could more than one test be used for my study?
4. Have the validity and reliability of the test I plan to use been established? Could they be established?
5. Have I used this test before? With what degree of success?
6. Will the test permit me to adequately address my research questions or hypotheses?
7. Do I know exactly how many tests I will need to have the proper sample for my study?
8. Can I control the administration of the test, to ensure the collection of high-quality data?
9. Could I use the test with other data-collection methods or techniques?
10. Is there an opportunity for me to pretest my data-collection process?

THE FOLLOWING QUESTIONS, RELATED TO YOUR SPECIFIC SCHOOL AND INTERESTS, ARE PRESENTED HERE TO GUIDE YOUR THINKING AND ACTION TOWARD THE SELECTION OF AN APPROPRIATE RESEARCH TOPIC.

1. What types of topics have been approved at your school?
2. What is the philosophy at your school on *when* you can start looking for your research topic?
3. Is there a graduate students' association (master's, doctoral, or other) that may be of assistance in finding a topic?
4. Are students permitted to attend doctoral or master's defenses at your school? At a nearby school?

5. Are there any organizations or groups in your area that might like to have research conducted that would meet your requirements?

6. What professional organizations meet regularly in your area? Are there any annual meetings scheduled for any professional organizations during the time that you will be conducting your research?

7. Does your school have copies of dissertation or thesis abstracts?

8. What general topic areas are of interest to members of the faculty? Of these, which are of interest to you?

9. Who, among the faculty, would you like to work with on the research?

10. Have you talked to students who have recently completed their research requirements?

THREE

Research Committee

The research committee has two roles to perform: the role of advisor and the role of judge. In its advisor role, the committee helps the student during the research phase of his work—from the development of an acceptable proposal through the completion of research. In its role of judge, the committee hears the student's oral defense of his dissertation and decides whether he has now completed the final requirement for the doctoral or master's degree.

During the research phase, committee members should be available to the student as often as needed. They should be a source of guidance and assistance to the student, developing his ability to conduct scholarly academic research. Each member should bring to the committee a different area of expertise that is desirable or required for the research. One member might bring the theoretical background needed for the study; another, the statistical expertise. Each should complement the other members, so that the student

28

has an effective team working with him toward the successful completion of the research effort. In essence, the student and committee are jointly working on the research.

At the oral defense of the dissertation, the committee may be supplemented by other members from the faculty or from outside the school or university. From a practical point of view, both the committee and the candidate are defending the research effort. For it is reasonable to assume that if the candidate has not conducted the research properly, the committee should share the responsibility for that failure.

What is the role of the research committee chairman?

The most influential man on your research committee, as well as the most knowledgeable man on the committee in the area being researched, will probably be the chairman. He will usually be the one you work with most closely. He will often coordinate your efforts with the other members of the committee and thus save you precious time. An important function of the research chairman is to represent you to the other members of the committee. He can say things to other faculty members that you cannot. Thus, it is important for you to develop a close working relationship and rapport with your chairman. He will largely determine whether you complete your dissertation.

Since your research committee chairman is critical to your success, be sure to select him with care (if you have the opportunity to select him). He should be a well-respected member of the faculty. He should be deeply interested in the topic. (He might even be the one who suggested the research topic.) He should be someone you respect, trust, and can work with, and who will return this respect, trust, and cooperative attitude.

Often the topic you select will dictate who must be the chairman. This can work for or against you. If the topic you might select dictates that a certain faculty member be the chairman, and you feel that he would be an ideal man for the position, then the topic is worth exploring. If the topic dictates a chairman whom you would not like to work with, then you might want to reevaluate and possibly drop the topic.

Will I be allowed to select my research committee? If so, whom should I try to get on the committee?

Schools vary widely in the latitude afforded the candidate in the selection of his committee. In some schools the entire committee is appointed. In others the candidate is permitted to approach any faculty member to request that he serve on his committee. Find out what your school's policy is and adhere to it. However, since you may be working with this committee for an extended period of time, you should—if at all possible—attempt to influence the selection of a committee that increases your chances of completing a high-quality research paper in the time you have allotted for the task.

If you will be using statistical-analysis techniques, try to get a statistician on the committee. This can prevent false starts and might save time and effort in the data-analysis stage. It also might make the defense easier, when questions are asked about your methods of analysis.

If a faculty member is well known in the area you are researching, then he should be on your committee from the beginning. If he is unable to serve on the research committee, he should at least be consulted during the various stages of the dissertation process. This consultation should, of course, be cleared through your committee. In general, you should try to draw from faculty expertise even though those having relevant knowledge are not members of your committee. What is your committeee's feeling on this matter?

Be especially alert to the possibility that potential committee members are going on sabbaticals or might be leaving the university for an extended period of time. Try to determine which faculty members will be at the university during the time that you are writing the dissertation. It is easy to lose a semester or a year of time when a committee member is not available. Do your best to avoid this loss.

Finally, the members of your committee should be a *harmonious* group with a *very active* interest in your topic. Generally speaking, the individual members should share a common basis of thinking regarding the topic and should feel that they can work with the other members in an atmosphere of mutual harmony. When members of the committee develop antagonistic or hostile viewpoints, and refuse to work and cooperate with other members, the candidate is the one who suffers. Try to get a committee that will be able to work together on your behalf during the entire research time. Be aware of situations that might develop into personality clashes within the committee and try to prevent them from disrupting committee member relationships. In these situations, an effective chairman is most valuable.

Who has to approve my research proposal—the entire committee or only the chairman?

The answer depends upon the policies in effect at your school, and you should be able to find out by a call to the doctoral office. But even if only the chairman is required to approve the proposal, it is still to your benefit to *obtain signatures of approval from all members of the committee*. If, for instance, there is a change in your committee at a later date, you will have solid evidence that the topic was initially acceptable to the entire committee. Furthermore, if you do not have this unanimous approval, one or more of your committee members may later complain, "I did not approve this topic; if I had been consulted, I would have given you my reasons at that time."

*HERE ARE A FEW QUESTIONS ABOUT RESEARCH COM-
MITTEES AT YOUR SCHOOL.*

1. How many members are on the research committee?

2. How are these members chosen?

3. What influence can you have over the selection process?

4. Which faculty member would you most like to have on your research committee?

5. Which faculty member would you least like to have on your research committee?

6. Must all members of the committee be from the school or department in which you are earning your degree?

7. Can members be selected from outside the university?

8. What is the role of the research committee chairman? What authority and responsibility does he have?

9. Is the research committee the same group that conducts the defense? If not, how is the defense committee selected?

10. Can the research committee chairman select the other members?

11. How closely do the members of the committee normally work? Does the student work most with the chairman?

12. Can the chairman add members to the committee or remove members from the committee?

13. Can the research committee chairman keep this position if he leaves the university?

14. What kind of committee would be best for you?

FOUR

Research Proposal

The research proposal delineates the specific area of your research. It should state the purpose, scope, methodology, overall organization, and limitations of your study and define any special terms that may be unique to your study. It could include a review of the relevant material written on the topic and should indicate how your research will make a contribution to the field and where you differ from the research conducted by others in the same general area.

It should also include a tentative table of contents of the final report. This is a critical part of the dissertation proposal. For if you cannot at this stage clearly visualize the general organization of your final report, then you probably do not know precisely where you are going. You may change the table of contents prior to the final report, and probably will, but at least you should be heading in a specific direction when the change is dictated. Lack of direction is one of the most prevalent causes of inconclusive and incom-

33

plete research at the graduate level. The proposal should represent a clear path from the statement of your research questions or hypotheses to the ultimate completion of the written report.

The proposal will also suggest a possible research committee, since the area of specialty in which you are writing usually dictates which members of the faculty should logically be on the research committee.

Also, the proposal may serve as the basis of your final report. The first two or three chapters of your dissertation could be contained in the proposal, after you have made possible modifications and expansions.

What benefits should I expect from a well-prepared research proposal?

A properly prepared research proposal will help you to think out the critical issues involved in your research; lay the foundation for your research; help you to look for and isolate pending problems and therefore, if some of these problems prove unsolvable, enable you to drop the topic before spending an inordinate amout of time on it; permit you to use your time more efficiently and effectively once the research is underway; serve as a "road map" for your research, always letting you know where you have been and where you are going; serve as a "contract" with the school (depending upon the policies in effect there); force you to think through the entire process, thus providing you with an integrated approach to the research.

The proposal is an important step in the thesis or dissertation process. It should not be viewed as constricting or restrictive or as a needless waste of time. Prepare your proposal well, and you will have little chance of becoming lost in the work. You will also have a better chance of selling the topic to the research committee. You should feel more confident once you have taken a critical look at your entire project and have received the benefit of comments from members of the research committee in looking for potential problems.

Even if the proposal is a formality at your school, it should not be treated as a mere formality by you. You have much to lose by taking such an approach, and probably very little to gain. And you should never consider the time spent on the proposal as wasted. There may be some minor inconveniences, but in the long run the more time you spend in planning for your research, the more swiftly and smoothly the entire process should be for you.

The proposal should lay out a clear path from the statement of your research questions or hypotheses to the ultimate completion of the written report. If there are going to be any stumbling blocks or problems in your research efforts, find out what they are now, before it may be too late. A major problem (such as data not being available) could occur after you have invested months of time on the topic, and you could be forced to abandon it. This should not happen if you plan the research properly, by clearly outlining and testing all aspects of the topic in the preparation of the proposal. Do not make the common mistake of assuming that there will be some way of handling the problem later. Face the possibility now. Once you are virtually certain that no major problem will crop up to force abandonment of the topic, you can proceed with much greater confidence.

What should I include in my research proposal?

There is a wide range of what is expected in a proposal, and only what is acceptable at your school is important to you. Perhaps there are copies of accepted proposals that you can review. If your school has no formal requirements, the following Sample Proposal Format may suggest a beginning.* You might also be interested in developing policies and procedures that seem to you most desirable

* This format, developed by faculty members of the School of Government and Business Administration at George Washington University, is made available to each graduate student in the school.

for developing proposals. If there is a doctoral or master's students' association at the school, this might be a project worth undertaking —the formulation of a set of guidelines for preparing acceptable proposals.

SAMPLE PROPOSAL FORMAT

1. Routine information

    A. Name

    B. Addresses (home and business addresses and telephone numbers)

    C. College (college or school in which registered)

    D. Degree (degree sought through program)

    E. Major advisor of research

    F. Research advisory committee members

    G. Dissertation title

    H. Date

2. Research question

    A. Subject area (recognized general subject of research question)

    B. Research question (major question, concept, or hypothesis to be dealt with)

    C. Subsidiary questions (questions to be answered to answer research question)

    D. Discussion (of significance of research question)

    E. Limitations (study constraints)

    F. Anticipated contribution

3. Methodology

    A. Information (general kind of information to be used)

    B. Sources (sources from which information is to be secured; related research attempted by others)

    C. Collection (methodology by which information is to be collected)

4. Chapter outline

Preliminary chapter titles and content summaries

5. Bibliography

A preliminary list in bibliographic form of material relevant to the research

6. Time schedule

The time schedule for execution of the dissertation research project is to be stated in terms of actual dates. Scheduling should begin with the total time available from the date the project is to be initiated to the date the final copy of the dissertation must be submitted in order to qualify for graduation on the desired convocation date.

    A. Research and preparation of first preliminary draft copy

    B. First review by major advisor

    C. Revision of first preliminary draft copy

    D. Preparation and review of subsequent preliminary draft copies

    E. Preparation of final draft copy

    F. Review by dissertation committee

    G. Preparation of final copy

    H. Proofreading of final copy

    I. Approval by major advisor and dissertation committee and request for oral examination

    J. Oral examination

    K. Submission of final copies

Must the research proposal be defended?

Some schools do require that the proposal be defended. At these schools the committee that will supervise the research meets with the candidate to have him present the proposed research topic in detail. The candidate is then asked questions by the research committee to clarify any points, to suggest areas that may be included in the study, and to reach an agreement on the validity of the topic and the data-collection and data-analysis techniques. In short, the purpose of the proposal defense is to ascertain whether the topic is one that merits scholarly research at the thesis or dissertation level.

If the proposal is successfully defended, the candidate should be able to begin his research with the feeling that he has a topic that is manageable and a committee that understands what he is trying to accomplish. After a proposal defense has been conducted, there should be little chance of a major disaster later on. That is why it is best to openly face the committee in advance of the research. Far better to kill a topic in a dissertation proposal defense than to invest months of effort and then abandon the topic.

If your school requires a proposal defense, attend one or more of these defenses to prepare for your own or to assist you in determining what is required for an acceptable proposal at your school. If no defense is required, suggest a meeting with your research committee to defend your proposal before you commit yourself to the topic. Try to get the approval of all committee members at this meeting.

If I have successfully defended my dissertation proposal, do I have a contract with the school that my topic is acceptable for a dissertation?

A proposal that is successfully defended should represent a type of contract with the school. With this contract should come an obligation on the part of the school to consider it an acceptable topic even if the chairman of your research committee leaves, or the committee is changed, before you have completed the final report. In fact, that is the reason for the suggestion that you defend the proposal even if it is not required at your school. It might give you an added measure of protection should you need it after a committee change.

If there is a doctoral students' association at your school, you might suggest that the idea of a contract be discussed with the faculty and incorporated into any existing policies governing doctoral and master's research work.

Should my hypotheses or research questions be spelled out in the proposal, or could they be put in final form after the proposal is completed?

The proposal should contain all hypotheses or research questions, stated precisely as they will appear in the final report. Some schools require that these hypotheses be identically worded in the proposal and the final report. You should want this requirement, since it gives you added assurance that the nature of the research, as spelled out in your approved proposal, will not be *materially* changed at the time you are making the final writing of the report.

You will probably find that stating hypotheses or research questions is a difficult task. However, spend all the time you can to get them properly worded. Do not proceed until you are certain that your research questions, as you have them formulated, indicate precisely what you intend to do. You will be rewarded at the later stages of your research.

Since we are on the topic of hypotheses, your hypotheses should appear at least three places: (1) in your proposal, under a section probably called "Questions to Be Researched" or "Hypotheses to Be Tested"; (2) in the first chapter of the final report, under a section with a similar heading; (3) in that chapter of your

39

final report where the hypotheses or research questions are discussed. Relating your hypotheses in this manner should show that you are organized and will keep the reader aware of the central focus of your research at all times. It prevents the reader from searching the paper for the hypotheses, or from misinterpreting the nature of your research effort.

Is it permissible for me to deviate from my original proposal while I am conducting my research?

Depending upon the nature of the change, it may be permissible and should even be expected. A severe deviation should not be expected, but some change will almost always be required. The proposal represents as clear a charter of your proposed efforts as you could establish without actually conducting the research. But something unexpected in the data collection, analysis, or interpretation may necessitate *minor* changes—for instance, in the scope of your work, in the format of the final report, or in the number of chapters.

Some schools insist that the final report must not deviate at all from the proposal. This requirement seems unrealistic and too stringent, since it gives no latitude to the research committee to enrich the research by insights or knowledge produced at a later stage in the research process. But check with your school's requirements. The more stringent the requirements are with reference to the proposal, the more effort you must put into preparation of the proposal.

If I do deviate slightly from my original proposal, must I revise it and get approval of the changes?

This procedure varies from school to school. Normally, the original proposal, once approved, is not revised even though many changes are made as research progresses. If changes are significant, then it might be advisable to write a letter to your committee (get a copy in your file), explaining how the changes differ from the original proposal. If necessary, you may even have the committee members sign the letter as an indication of their approval of the changes.

How do I get a proposal prepared and approved?

First, find out what the requirements are at your school. If written policies or procedures are available, this would be the best place to start. Next, find someone who has just recently gone through the proposal process and see if he will discuss his experiences with you. Or you could attend a proposal defense if these are open to doctoral students. Also, read the sections of this book relating to proposals. Then you should be ready to prepare your proposal.

If you have been able to use the proposal process for some of your term papers, then you should be familiar with the process. However, assuming that you are not familiar with proposal preparation, but the natural-selection method (a process whereby the student finds a professor who is interested in a topic that the student is interested in developing into a dissertation topic, and works with that professor in developing a proposal) exists for finding a research committee chairman, I would suggest this approach. Meet with the professor that you would like to have as chairman of your committee and seek his ideas of what should be included in a proposal. Then, assuming that you have discussed the nature of the topic and are in agreement, develop a proposal in accordance with the guidance he has given. Take this tentative proposal to him to get his comments. Continue this process until you have incorporated his suggestions, plus the results of your own investigations, into the contents of the proposal. Then you should be ready to discuss the proposal with the complete research committee to get guidance from them.

THE FOLLOWING QUESTIONS, DIRECTLY RELATED TO YOUR SCHOOL, SHOULD BE OF ASSISTANCE IN GUIDING YOUR THINKING TOWARD THE PROPER DEVELOPMENT OF AN ACCEPTABLE PROPOSAL.

1. What is the purpose of the proposal at your school? Is it a formality, or is an acceptable proposal one that takes considerable time to prepare?

2. Are there guidelines for preparing the proposal?

3. Does the proposal have to be defended? Can it be defended if the student wishes to?

4. Is the proposal considered a contract between the school and the student?

5. Must the entire research committee approve the proposal, or does the chairman handle this himself?

6. How rigid is the proposal? That is, how much, if any, are you permitted to deviate from the proposal after your research is underway?

7. If you do deviate from the proposal, must the proposal be revised?

8. What is the normal method for getting a proposal approved at your school?

9. Are copies of approved proposals available for students to review?

10. Does the proposal normally represent the major portion of the first three chapters of the dissertation or thesis?

FIVE

Data Collection and Analysis

Once a topic has been selected to research, then data must be collected and analyzed in preparation for the final report. This is perhaps the most critical step in the dissertation or thesis process. If the data cannot be collected, the research cannot be conducted.

Many graduate students, in their rush to get the proposal submitted and accepted, assume that they will be able to get the data somehow. Too often, however, the data is not available, or the student must overcome insurmountable problems to collect and analyze it. Thus, after spending a great deal of time on the topic, he finally has to abandon it. If there is a reasonable doubt that you will be able to get the required data, or if there are pending difficulties, then you should explore another topic.

How can I be sure that the data I collect are directly related to my hypotheses or research questions?

By whatever means required, you must make sure of the relevancy of your data. One such means is a *pretest* of your data-collection technique. That is, after you have collected a small sample, pretend that your test data is final and that you are going to complete your research. If you are unable adequately to test your hypotheses or research questions with the data you have (ignoring the small sample size), then you may not have collected the proper data. If you can relate the test data to the hypotheses, then you can be reasonably certain that the final data will be directly related to your hypotheses.

When you are preparing the questionnaire, or interview questions, or other methods of data collection, screen each item for its relevance to your hypotheses. Ask: "Of what value is this piece of information to the central purpose of my research?" Or "Why is this information needed; what will it add to the study?" Be extremely critical at this time. In some research you may never be able to return for the proper data if it is not captured on the first try. That is why a pretest of the data-collection process is important.

If you have several hypotheses or research questions, you may wish to assign each item of data to the particular question it is related to. You can thus see whether your questions are properly dispersed; that is, whether you have sufficient data related to each hypothesis or research question.

Before you start the collection process, you must know the precise method by which you will relate your data to your hypotheses; otherwise, you cannot be certain that you are collecting the proper data.

I know plenty of doctoral candidates with mountains of data, but they can't seem to complete their dissertations. Why?

Doctoral candidates with mountains of data generally have not clearly carved out their area of research. Mountains of data are not required to complete a dissertation, only sufficient amounts of *relevant* data, related to the stated purpose of your research. Candidates often use the "shotgun" approach, collecting everything that might be useful. Don't make this mistake. Don't collect unnecessary and useless data. Determine what data you need to test your research questions or hypotheses and collect that kind of data in sufficient quantity to complete your research.

The more data you have, the more confused you might get. And you may not be able to arrange all this material into a meaningful outline of research. Also, you may feel that since you have the data, you must use it—even when it will not fit into an organized pattern. So don't collect for the sake of collecting. Collect only relevant data.

What happens if I do not support my hypotheses or research questions? Will I have to start my dissertation over again?

You should not have to support your hypotheses or research questions in order to produce acceptable research. If your data does not support your hypotheses, then you are probably doing a real job of research. That is, if you are not able to warp the data to say what you want it to say, you probably have a dissertation worthy of publication. If, on the other hand, you are merely trying to *justify* hypotheses that you know to be correct, your findings very probably *will* support your hypotheses but will also very probably be trivial.

To ease your mind on this question, you probably should ask your research advisor and perhaps your entire committee how they feel about the possibility of your not being able to support your hypotheses. After all, they will be determining whether you complete your dissertation.

How can I eliminate my biases in data collection and analysis?

You cannot completely eliminate your bias; but you *can* recognize and reduce this bias to a manageable amount, where it does not influence your findings. As a matter of fact, you may be asked at the defense to describe the steps you took to eliminate your bias in the research.

One possible way to reduce bias is to use a validation or checking procedure on your analysis of the data. Assume, for example, that you are to read the narrative comments of respondents and produce categories, or to group the responses into predetermined categories. You can reduce bias by asking someone who is not familiar with your hypotheses to perform the same analysis you will be doing. Then you can statistically compare the two findings. If they do not differ statistically, you can either use your analysis or the independent one to produce your final results. (Check this process with your research advisor for his approval on the technique used.) Or you may decide to have an independent, unbiased outsider do the analysis. Properly handled, this procedure could give you a strong answer (at the defense) on the "reduction of bias" question. Naturally, the selection of the independent person must be handled with care, and your research committee should approve that person.

There are two other forms of bias that the researcher must contend with: *sampling bias* and *measurement bias*. Sampling bias might be introduced by the methods and techniques used to collect data. Measurement bias may result from the methods used to measure the data that is collected. Consult a statistical-analysis book to familiarize yourself with these sources of bias and to learn what you can do to minimize their influence on your research.

What is the difference between Interpretation *and* Analysis *of data?*

Once you have a mass of data, you normally begin to analyze it. Your analysis may result in the preparation of tables and graphs. You may then *describe* these tables and charts and, on the basis of your description, state that you have supported or rejected your hypotheses. If you do this, you may have missed an important step in the research process. For your research to be complete, you must do more than present and describe tables and charts containing data. You must also *interpret* the data—assess its *meaning* and relate this meaning to the purpose of your paper. When you have prepared a table and described it fully, ask yourself this question: "What does this table mean? What significance does it have, as related to the purpose of my research?"

Do I have to use statistical tests to analyze my data?

No, of course not. Many people shy away from the use of statistics for the same reason that they keep away from computers. But you don't need to be a statistician to use statistical tests, just as you don't need to be a computer programmer to use the computer. And there is much to say for the use of standard statistical tests in the analysis of data for research. A few of these reasons are given below.

First of all, assuming that you have collected your data properly and have used an appropriate statistical test, you will generally find it easier to defend your dissertation if you have analyzed the data by using an accepted statistical test and have supported or rejected your hypotheses on this basis. If you rely upon inference, inductive or deductive logic, or subjective judgment to support or reject your hypotheses, your conclusions may prove much more difficult to defend.

When you use statistical tests for your data, your research will give the appearance of being scholarly and rigorous. In fact, if used properly, these statistical tests *will* produce a more rigorous and scholarly research effort. Of course, I am not suggesting that you merely create an impression that the research is rigorous, even though the final report may be prejudged on appearance and little attention given to substance. But since your work could be prejudged, why not let it be prejudged in the right direction? Or, better still, why not have the substance *and* the appearance of a rigorous, scholarly research paper?

If I use statistical tests for analyzing my data, won't I have to defend my choice of tests?

Yes, you should be asked to defend it. Also, you should have no difficulty answering such a question at the defense. In the first place, your committee should include one member who has the degree of statistical sophistication required for your project. Realizing that the question may be asked, plan ahead by trying to get a statistically oriented person on the committee to discuss the various tests that might be used. Get the approval of your statistician for the test you use. His approval is often enough to justify the selection of a technique or method of analysis.

Be certain that the method of collecting the data and the method of analysis are *appropriate* for your research. Consider more than one technique and use more than one if this is appropriate. It may further strengthen your case at the defense. The fact that you are aware of other techniques and have considered them is often enough to answer the question of why you chose the one you used.

What tests have others used in similar research? The fact that you have used the same test—*if* the test is appropriate—may support your argument. Or you could use another test to lend variety to related research (when your research is similar to the work of others).

Can I use a computer in my research when I have only limited knowledge about computers?

Don't make the mistake of thinking that you have to be a computer expert to use the computer effectively in your research. Of course, it would be helpful if you did have such knowedge, but it isn't necessary. Only a limited amount of information is needed, and you can get it even if you know almost nothing about computers.

All you really need to know is what you can expect from the

computer and what information you have that is to be processed. Take this information with you as you consult the personnel at the computer center at your school (assuming that such a center exists); usually, they are happy to display their computer capability and will assist you willingly.

In many schools there are people at the computer center who have the specific job of assisting students and faculty members in using the computer for their research; in some schools computers are reserved for research use only. Too often the student is not aware of the vast potential available to him in the way of computer time (almost always free to full-time students) and personnel who know how the computer can be used in research.

There is a practical limitation to the amount of assistance you can reasonably expect from the computer staff. Don't expect them to complete the data analysis and send the completed reports to you. They should, however, be able to get some calculations for you on existing programs that can be modified by you to suit your requirements. Writing programs tailor-made to your research effort is another matter.

If programs have to be written, you may be able to hire a computer programmer; the computer center's personnel may be able to suggest someone. If your data has to be keypunched into cards for the computer (usually the case), you may have to hire a keypunch operator. The computer center's staff can assist you in designing the cards to hold the data and can even help you estimate the cost. For most research projects keypunch costs should be an insignificant item. But don't assume anything about these costs; find out specifically by asking someone to help you estimate them. It is a fairly simple process to estimate such costs.

If there are students who are learning how to write computer programs, you may be able to save the cost of hiring a computer programmer. Students in such classes are often very glad to get a real program to write, and the instructor is often just as glad to have these programs to assign. Or you may be able to use one of the "canned" programs that have been written. These programs, general purpose in nature, can often be used exactly as they are written to produce reports that give you all the data you need in statistical form. Many of these programs are designed to calculate standard statistical tests *once the data is in proper form for the computer.* Therefore, if you do plan to use the computer in your research, by all means consult the personnel at the computer center before you complete your questionnaire or data-collection technique. Proper design of these forms will often eliminate the need for writing a special program for your research, and may permit you to use the canned programs. Visit your computer center to see what canned programs are available and in what form the data is needed. Then, if you can, use some of these programs for term papers in preparation for the thesis or dissertation.

I want to learn about computers. How can I learn about them quickly?

It is now a relatively simple task to pick up the rudiments of computer programming. On the assumption that you want to know only enough to make profitable use of the computer for your research, here are some methods to gain familiarity with programming.

The best way to learn about computer programming is to write computer programs. If your school has a course in computer programming, you might want to take or audit the course; or you could ask the professor for permission to sit in on the course or, at least, the first few sessions, until you are able to write a simple program. Then you will have some basis for self-learning. Or you could use a programmed-instruction text on computer programming or even a computer that has been programmed to teach you how to program it. See whether such facilities are available at your school or at a school nearby.

You may discover that several other graduate students also want to learn about computers for their research. Perhaps a special class could be established that would meet for a few times (usually four to six sessions are sufficient), with all class material geared to precisely what you wish to know about the computer. Often, members of the computer center's staff conduct such sessions on an informal basis for faculty, staff, and students. Or perhaps a graduate student would be willing to establish an informal class and teach it for some of his fellow students. The advantage to this approach is that there are none of the stresses of a formal class, and the material that is covered can be directly related to the needs of the students.

Can I use already published data instead of generating the data myself?

The decision rests with your research committee or chairman. Some faculty members do not like this approach to academic research, since they feel that the student learns much more by collecting the data himself. But many fine dissertations have extended the range or interpretation of already existing data bases or have approached the data with a new slant or purpose.

The government publishes a huge amount of data. The Bureau of the Census and the Department of Labor are two major suppliers of data and statistical material that could be useful for a thesis or dissertation. Another potential source for your data would be associations of various kinds. Still another source could be organizations that specialize in the accumulation and dissemination of statistical and other information. Or someone else's thesis or dissertation may contain tables of statistical data that can be used as a thesis or dissertation extending the original research.

Can a questionnaire or an interview be used to collect data for a dissertation or thesis?

Although questionnaires and interviews are frequently used for theses and dissertations, some faculty members will not permit their use because, they claim, the researcher is too biased to collect any data that would be valid or reliable. However, reliability of data is more a function of proper planning than of the technique used to collect that data. Of course, data from a questionnaire may not be reliable, but the same could be said for data collected by any other method if improper collection techniques are used. On the other hand, data may be extremely reliable when collected by using a properly designed, pretested, and properly administered questionnaire.

How can I construct an effective questionnaire?

The proper design of questionnaires for scholarly research is a difficult and complex procedure. Much has been written about it. Here are a few hints (not in order of importance).

1. The *length* of your questionnaire is critical to the success of your data collection. The longer the form, the more reluctance to respond there is on the part of the potential respondent. Also, after completing part of a lengthy questionnaire, a respondent may tire and not put his best effort in responding to the latter part of the form. Therefore, if you *must* use a long questionnaire, try to place questions that are easily answered, and which have definitive answers, at the end of the form.

2. Try to reduce to a minimum the time required to complete the form. In your pretesting of the questionnaire, determine the average time required to answer all questions. State this either at the top of the first page of the form or in the cover letter, or in both places. The less time time required to complete the questionnaire, the higher return rate you can expect.

3. Reducing the number of pages makes it appear that less time will be required to complete the form. In other words, people will think that a two-page questionnaire takes less time to complete than a three-page one. Of course, this may not be true, but you can create this illusion. To create the illusion of less time to complete, these items might be considered. Whenever possible (for instance, with multiple-choice questions, true-false, yes-no, or single-

word answers), list the alternatives across rather than down the page, or place the alternatives on the same line as the question. In addition, consider single spacing instead of double spacing, or reduce the amount of space between questions or sections of the questionnaire, or photocopy to cut the size of the final product. Once the respondent has started completing the questionnaire, he is likely to complete it. Getting him started is the problem, and the illusion of its being short will help.

4. Many people are reluctant to state their salary or other personal information, including age. If these factors are required in your study, then you may reduce the resistance by using categories that conceal a *specific* response. For example, a respondent may let you know that his salary is between $10,000 and $15,000, but he may be reluctant to specify it as exactly $13,500. The use of categories is actually beneficial to you, since it may be more useful to analyze data by groups than by specifics.

5. If a personal piece of information is not necessary for your study, omit it from the form. Including it may reduce the response rate. Seek only information that is required to complete your research.

6. Pretest the questionnaire if at all possible. Pretesting is a very useful way of catching confusing and unclear questions prior to the actual data-collection process. The very fact that you have pretested the questionnaire will be useful at the defense, when a faculty member asks what you did to ensure the reliability and validity of your data. If you have pretested to eliminate any misleading aspect of the questionnaire, you will feel more comfortable with your final report and with the data that you are using in your analysis and interpretation. In addition, you will probably gain insights into the data-collection process during the pretest. These insights might include methods for improving the rate of return. Thus, you will be in a position to formulate written or oral instructions on the basis of the pretest results. Another value from pretesting is that you have a sample of your data that you can use to test the analysis and interpretation parts of your proposed research.

7. Word each question as simply, clearly, straightforwardly,

and briefly as possible. Your pretest should help in determining the most effective wording of the questions.

8. Be aware of the "central-tendency" concept; that is, the tendency of people to avoid taking an extreme stand and to choose the "middle" answer on a question. If, for instance, you have a question with an odd number of choices (usually three or five), there is a tendency for respondents to select the middle response. One approach to the central-tendency problem is to use an even number of categories for your questions, thereby forcing the respondent to take one side or the other.

9. If appropriate for your research, favor the use of closed-end questions; that is, questions with a specific number of answers, from which the respondent selects one or more. This method simplifies the analysis process, particularly if you are going to use the computer for analysis of the data.

10. If you have questions that contain several possible responses (for example, five), and the respondent may choose *one or more,* expect some difficulty in analyzing the data. Since many combinations are possible, you must be prepared to analyze all of these possibilities. Thus, a respondent might select items 2 and 4, or 3 and 5, or any combination up to an including *all* or *none* of the choices. If your research requires questions with the possibility of multiple selections, of course you should use such questions; just recognize the analysis problem in your planning and proceed. Do not sacrifice quality of data for ease in analysis.

11. Include demographic factors (such as age, sex, marital status, salary, seniority, location, position) if appropriate and relevant to your research. These factors multiply the number of possibly useful tables and permit you to sharpen the focus of your data analysis. You may even uncover findings that you did not anticipate (findings that you can include in a separate chapter on "Other Findings"). Or these factors could suggest areas for additional research, a section often contained in the final chapter of the written report.

12. Relate each question on the form to the purpose of your

research or to some specific chapter in your proposed table of contents. If a question cannot be readily related, consider dropping it from the questionnaire. This will shorten the form and enable you to keep your attention on the central purpose of your research.

13. Anticipate what you will do with the data once you have it in your hands. Unless you know exactly what you will do with each piece of data, you cannot be sure that you are collecting the proper data. Your pretest can help in this respect. Pretend that the test data is your final data, and prepare sample reports that are identical to the ones that will appear in your final report.

14. Seek the advice of any of your friends who have used a questionnaire recently.

15. Consider carefully the sequence in which the questions appear on the questionnaire. Do you want the "easy" questions first or last? Do some questions logically belong together? If some questions are together, will they tend to distort the data; that is, will the answer on one question tend to influence the answer on another question? Is this something you want to happen? Will a resequencing of the questions permit you to shorten the questionnaire? Use logic in sequencing the questions.

16. If possible, build an internal-consistency check into the questionnaire (for example, two questions that should be answered in a similar or an opposite manner). The consistency check *cannot* ensure reliable data, but it is a step in that direction. If you use this consistency check, the "consistency questions" should probably be well separated on the form, not even appearing on the same page.

17. Put yourself in the place of the respondent. What will motivate him to complete the questionnaire for you? What may prompt him to react adversely, or to fail to respond? Try out your questionnaire on some of your friends if you can rely upon them to give you critical comments.

If you plan to use a questionnaire, spend considerable time on its design. Use term papers as opportunities to practice the design and use of questionnaires. What better way to develop skill in questionnaire design than to design and use them? For additional information on questionnaires, an excellent book is *Questionnaire*

Design and Attitude Measurement, by A. N. Oppenheim (New York: Basic Books, 1966).

Where can I find people to complete my questionnaire or to provide data in some other form?

When people get together, you have a potential source of dissertation data; and a *captive audience* may be waiting for you. What groups meet in your city or your geographic area? Are there any state, regional, or national conventions or association meetings planned for the time when you will be seeking sources of data? Which associations meet in your locality? Are there any that might be available to you as a result of your relationships with these organizations?

The use of captive audiences has certain advantages over, say, a mailing. In the first place, you can *control the data-collection process* well; and the validity and reliability of data increase with the amount of control you are able to exercise in the collection procedure. Furthermore, captive audiences provide *immediate responses,* in contrast to a questionable response over a considerable time period in the mailing approach. When the group leaves the collection area or room, you normally have data ready for analysis. Since almost everyone in the room will respond after you have given instructions, you could increase the response rate to practically 100 percent. In a mailing, you can anticipate a response of perhaps 30 percent to 40 percent. This single feature of the captive-audience approach may be sufficient reason to use the technique to collect data.

Even more important than the high response rate is the *quality of data* that you should receive. You should be able to give instructions in a uniform manner to all groups. If more than one group is needed, one person should address all groups. This person will be able to clarify any misunderstanding "on the spot," thus increasing the amount of useful data that you receive.

The most obvious disadvantage is that the captive-audience technique cannot be used if you must conduct interviews on a personal basis. Another drawback is that you must have the *proper facilities* to conduct the sessions. No facilities are required for a mailing. If you are gathering your data from one or more organizations and they do not have the facilities for a large group, you may have to break the total sample into small groups, thereby necessitating several repetitions of the instructions. Perhaps another disadvantage is the *amount of control required*. Since each person should get the complete set of instructions, you may have to close off the room you are using and permit no one to enter once the instructions are underway. This may present some problems if the person who is late is of high status in the organization.

In general, however, if it is properly planned, the captive-audience approach will permit you to capture a huge amount of data in a relatively short period of time. In one day, or easily within one week, you may be able to collect all the data required for your research. This means that the data-collection phase of the research, already established as very critical to your success, can be completed very swiftly by the use of captive audiences.

I plan to administer a questionnaire to a group (or several groups) of respondents. How can I conceal their identity so that they will feel free to give me reliable and truthful data?

There is no way to convince everyone that his identity will be concealed, but there are several steps that should convince most respondents. Here are a few hints that might be helpful.

1. Explain the entire procedure that you are using to preserve the identity of the respondents.

2. If possible, do not know who is coming to the room at any particular session (if you are conducting several similar sessions), and do not permit anyone to enter the room after the instructions are underway. Permit people to switch sessions if they want to.

3. Do not hand a questionnaire to any respondent (it may be marked), and do not accept a completed questionnaire from any respondent. Instead, let all respondents place their completed questionnaire on a desk or chair, on their way out of the room. Suggest that they place their questionnaires any place on the stack of completed ones. It might be advisable to have the first one who is

finished wait until two or three others have completed their questionnaires, so that they can all leave as a group. Do not look at the completed questionnaires until all of them have been placed on the stack. Tell respondents that you will not pick up the forms until all of them have been completed.

4. Let respondents sit wherever they want to in the room; if anyone thinks that the seats may be marked, have him exchange seats with someone else in the room.

5. Place a stack of blank questionnaires on each table or desk, or have one large stack from which each person can select. Have each person select a questionnaire for himself, and do not restrict him to taking the next one on top. If questionnaires are placed at tables, make sure that more questionnaires are provided than there are seats for the table. This gives each person an opportunity to select any questionnaire. When each person has his questionnaire, say that it is permissible to trade with a neighbor.

6. If the data is being collected within an organization, do not let people in the organization see the completed questionnaire in its original form. Let them see the results in summary form. If open-ended questions are contained on the questionnaire, the responses could be paraphrased and classified before the results are given to the organization.

7. If possible, let respondents know that they will see the summary results of your study. This encourages them to give useful information and helps remove the mystery of what you are going to do with the data.

8. Do not let respondents identify themselves to you, and try not to be able to identify any questionnaire for any respondent.

If I am collecting data from questionnaires or interviews, how do I know whether the people are telling the truth or merely what they think I want to hear?

If the information is factual, and you can verify the facts, then you are capable of determining whether the data you have gathered is true. If the data is largely of the opinion type, or depends upon the interpretation of the respondent, then there is no way to prove conclusively that the person is telling the truth.

Follow-up interviews may give you further insights into the usefulness of your data. A clear attempt to preserve the anonymity of the respondent in certain types of research is another method of increasing the reliability of the data you have collected.

I will be using a mailing procedure to collect my data. What are the advantages of this procedure? What problems should I anticipate?

Properly planned and administered, the mailing technique for collecting data can be very effective. You may be able to get data from a widely dispersed geographic region that would be prohibitively expensive with personal interviews or captive audiences. Furthermore, if you need or wish to have a large sample size, then you may have a better chance with a mailing. But an effective mailing, one that produces a high response rate with very reliable data, requires a significant amount of preplanning. Once the letters are placed in the mailbox, the process is out of your hands. Therefore, the success of the approach is completely dependent upon your skill in preparing the mailing.

The feeling of loss of control is the big worry to a person using the mails to collect his data. "What happens if I get no response?" is a question each person must ask himself. Such an event could happen, in which case you will suffer a real setback in your research. Or, assuming that you get some response, the persons who do reply may take their time about it. Do not expect every person to be as anxious to return his completed form as you were to send it to him. Many (most) will not respond at all.

With the large number of nonrespondents, you will have to address the problem of respondent bias; that is, did the persons who responded represent the total population to which the letters were sent? Or is there some bias introduced into the study by the nature and characteristics of those that responded?

When you make a mailing, you normally must include in your covering letter all the instructions that a respondent will get.

This means that the instructions must be made very clear and explicit. This, in turn, suggests that a careful pretesting of the instructions should have been conducted. Moreover, it is difficult to anticipate all areas of confusion or to clarify them by the written instructions.

It is easy to code forms that are sent in the mail, and potential respondents know this. For that reason, you may have a difficult time convincing them that their identity will remain unknown. If the anonymity of the respondent is important, this will increase the nonresponse rate. One question about salary may be enough to prevent the entire form from being completed.

Other factors might limit the number of responses you receive. People regularly receive a supply of junk mail each day. When your questionnaire arrives, it may quickly be classified as junk mail and discarded immediately. Or it could put the potential respondent in an uncooperative frame of mind, and he may intentionally send in erroneous information, thus affecting the validity and reliability of the data received from the mailing.

If you have a long questionnaire (to be defined by your research committee), you increase the likelihood of nonrespondents in a mailing. Thus, the size of the questionnaire may make mailing hazardous to your data-collection process.

It may be difficult, or impossible, to follow up on a mailing. With a small list, and using follow-up techniques, you may be able to make a second mailing. With a high nonrespondent rate and the difficulty of following up, the mailing approach has a double hazard.

Obviously, then, there are many difficulties with the use of the mails as a procedure for collecting data. It is important that you become aware of these serious drawbacks to the method. Then, if you must use the mails, you can take steps to minimize the difficulties.

What is an acceptable return rate for a mailing? How can I increase this return rate?

There is no generally acceptable return rate; that must be decided by your committee. When you are satisfied that you have received all of the questionnaires that you will be receiving, and that the returns are "enough" to proceed, you have reached the acceptable rate. Normally speaking, you should expect to receive at least 30 percent to 40 percent of the questionnaires. Using this assumed percent of returns, you should be able to forecast the number of questionnaires you must mail in order to receive the sample size you have agreed upon for your study.

The return rate is so variable that the percentages given above are only very rough guidelines. You can increase the percentage of returns if you plan and prepare properly. For a comprehensive coverage of the process and techniques of mailing questionnaires, an excellent reference book is *Professional Mail Surveys,* by Paul L. Erdos (New York: McGraw-Hill, 1970). Here are a few techniques that may be appropriate for you.

1. Design the questionnaire in such a fashion that you are able to encourage respondents to complete it. Try to relate to the potential respondents, and answer this question, before it is asked: "Why should I respond?"

2. Ask yourself who should receive your questionnaires? Use care in the selection process, so that the form goes to those most likely to respond.

3. Determine the proper time to make the mailing. Depending upon who your audience is, there are good and bad times to receive questionnaires.

4. Establish a reasonable deadline for the return of the questionnaire. An open date does not encourage a response. An unrealistic return date may irritate the potential respondent. In setting a realistic deadline, consider vacation schedules and seasonal demands on your particular respondents.

5. Use a follow-up letter if this technique is appropriate for the type of study you are conducting.

6. Identify yourself as a doctoral student if, after a discussion with your research chairman, you believe such identification will increase the rate of return.

7. Consider including an appropriate cover letter from you or your research chairman or someone who might carry some weight with the respondent.

8. Keep the questionnaire to a reasonable length.

9. If feasible, offer potential respondents a summary of your findings—a copy of your dissertation abstract, or a special summary prepared for respondents.

10. Consider using the school's stationery (with permission) or any other "official" stationery that might improve your chances for increasing the return rate.

THE FOLLOWING QUESTIONS, RELATED TO YOUR SCHOOL AND INTERESTS, ARE PRESENTED HERE TO GUIDE YOUR THINKING IN THE DATA-COLLECTION AND DATA-ANALYSIS PHASE OF YOUR RESEARCH.

1. Does the school favor the collection of original data or the use of already published data?

2. Are there major sources of data unique to your area? Would these sources be acceptable for a dissertation or thesis?

3. Is there a computer center on campus?

4. Is the computer center available for students? How can you get assistance in using the computer? What is the cost?

5. Does the school favor objective research, or is the emphasis upon subjective studies?

6. Is the use of data collected by means of a survey (questionnaire or interview) acceptable at your school?

7. What is the attitude of the faculty (the members that you will probably be working with) concerning the use of the mail for data collection?

8. Does the faculty favor the use of research questions or hypotheses for the thesis or dissertation.

9. Are there captive audiences in your area that might be good sources of data for your research?

10. What is the opinion of the faculty on the use of statistical tests?

Data Collection and Analysis

11. Do the faculty members believe that the data collected *must* support the research questions or hypotheses?

12. What sources of data have provided the basis for dissertations and theses at your school?

13. What techniques for data collection have been used for theses and dissertations at the school?

SIX

Writing the
Research Report

Your research project—no matter how well conceived—will receive little or no recognition or approval unless it is communicated to the research committee in a well-structured, comprehensive, and cohesive manner. The final report should be so constructed that the research committee can quickly grasp the essence of your efforts with a minimum of delay and searching. If the committee has to search to find out what you have accomplished, then you have not prepared your written report in an acceptable manner.

Good writing is hard work. It does not come easily to many people. And good writing requires rewriting. But if you will prepare yourself for the task by the gradual process of writing papers of increasing length, then the final research report will not become an insurmountable task. Properly organized and prepared, you should be able to produce an acceptable paper, of high quality, with a minimum of false starts and wasted motions.

Is there any general pattern of organization for research papers?

There are as many ways to organize your research as there are types of dissertations and theses. However, the following general format for a table of contents might assist you in organizing your research report. Many other equally useful approaches could be taken (as you will find by reviewing the tables of contents of theses and dissertations approved at your school for topics similar to yours).

TABLE OF CONTENTS, GENERAL FORMAT

Chapter 1   PURPOSE AND ORGANIZATION

> Purpose of the study
> Hypotheses or research questions
> Scope of the study
> Limitations
> Definition of terms
> Organization of the report

Chapter 2   REVIEW OF RELATED RESEARCH

> (Prepare an organized review of related and relevant research, indicating how your research will make a contribution)

Chapter 3 DATA COLLECTION AND ANALYSIS
> Methods used to collect data
> Method used to analyze data
> Validation or pretesting procedures

Chapter 4 (ADDRESSES RESEARCH QUESTION/
HYPOTHESIS 1)

Chapter 5 (ADDRESSES RESEARCH QUESTION/
HYPOTHESIS 2)

Chapter 6 (ADDRESSES RESEARCH QUESTION/
HYPOTHESIS 3)

Chapter 7 SUMMARY OF OTHER FINDINGS
> (Include in this chapter any findings that you think
> should be included in the final report but that may not
> have been anticipated or planned as a part of the study)

Chapter 8 SUMMARY AND SUGGESTIONS FOR
ADDITIONAL RESEARCH
> Summary and conclusions
> Suggestions for additional research
> Implications (indicate what group, theory, organization,
> discipline might be able to profit from your research)

BIBLIOGRAPHY (in the format required by your school)

APPENDICES (in the format required by your school)

The following comments discuss the content and purpose of each chapter in the final report, in generalized fashion. Obviously, you will have to modify these ideas to fit your particular topic.

Chapter 1 sets the stage for the report. It should include a statement of the purpose for which you undertook your research effort. It should spell out in specific terms the precise nature of your hypotheses, if you are using them, or give the general and any subsidiary research questions. It should outline the scope of your study and include any limitations on what you have done. If you are using terms that have a unique meaning in the context of your research, these should be defined in this chapter. (If there are a sufficient number of these terms, a separate appendix could be developed.) Another item often contained in Chapter 1 is a section called "Organization of the Study." This section—a paragraph or two on each chapter, indicating the contents in brief narrative— gives the reader the impression that you are well organized and assists him in assessing the contents of your paper.

Chapter 2 contains a review of *relevant* research, indicating why and how your work will make a contribution to the existing field of knowledge. The similarity and difference between your work and that of other authors in the field should be highlighted. This chapter may have resulted from term papers that you have written on your topic, or could have been part of your thesis if the topic is similar. Make the review of the literature relevant to your work. This simplifies your research and gives a clearer focus to your work.

Keep the size of this chapter to manageable proportions. No number of pages can be precisely stated, but a maximum of thirty pages is a number to work with. (As with all such estimates, there is plenty of room for deviation, depending upon the nature of your topic.) Don't expand the chapter by including data and material with only a casual relationship to your work.

After the reader has read this chapter, he should be aware of the current state of the literature, and he should know what you will be doing to extend the state of that knowledge. Incidentally, your summation of pertinent literature is often a significant contribution to knowledge and could be mentioned as one of your contributions at the dissertation defense. In fact, dissertations are written that crystallize and summarize the state of knowledge in a given field.

Chapter 3 discusses the methods and techniques used to

collect and analyze your data. If the techniques you used are relatively standard, you may not need a separate chapter to describe them. You could include this information in Chapter 1 or in an appendix or in the chapter or chapters where you specifically address your research questions or hypotheses. Wherever you discuss your methods, be sure to emphasize that your data is appropriate, reliable, valid, and usable and that your method of analysis is appropriate for the data you have. Describe any methods you used to ensure the validity, reliability, and usability of your data. The reader should be satisfied that your research report is based on solid data that was appropriately analyzed.

After Chapter 3, the table of contents can take many forms. For ease in presentation, let us assume that you have developed three research questions or three hypotheses. You should be able to modify what follows to your topic.

Chapter 4 addresses the first research question and any related or subsidiary questions. This chapter would contain an analysis of the data you used to test the question, an interpretation of the data, and your conclusions regarding this hypothesis or research question. These conclusions would indicate that you have either supported or rejected your research question. The reader should be made aware of what you have accomplished, in light of what you were attempting to do. A summary should be included at the end (or beginning) of the chapter (and in every other chapter where it appears to be appropriate).

Chapter 5 addresses the second research question or hypotheses and any related or subsidiary questions. This chapter could be similar to Chapter 4 in structure and format. A summary should be included at the end (or beginning) of the chapter.

Chapter 6 addresses the third research question or hypothesis and any related or subsidiary questions. The structure and format could be similar to the structure and format of Chapters 4 and 5.

You may have uncovered information that you think should be discussed, but for which you had not formulated a hypothesis or research question. A separate chapter could be devoted to these findings.

Chapter 7 could contain anything else that you think should be included in the final report. Having this chapter permits you to restrict your discussions in preceding chapters to specific research questions, and may prevent you from deviating from the subject in these earlier chapters. Knowing that you have a place in the final report (this chapter) for related, significant, or interesting findings often gives you the reason to omit it from a prior chapter.

The final chapter should contain at least three items: (1) *a summary and conclusions section* that briefly discusses what you have attempted to do and the results you have achieved (you may restate your original research questions or hypotheses and indicate whether you have supported or rejected them); (2) *suggestions for additional research* (a section indicating what questions you were unable to answer or what research questions you formulated as a result of your research); (3) an *indication of the usefulness of the research* (Who could benefit from what you have done? How? What theories, disciplines, organizations, groups, etc. would like to know what you have uncovered or concluded? What is the value of your effort?). The final chapter should not introduce any new data or analysis into the report. Everything that was to be tested or evaluated should have been included in prior chapters. Only a summation of your findings appears in the final chapter, making it relatively brief.

Of course, you will probably have a *bibliography* and *appendices* in your report. Keep your bibliography relevant. Don't pad this part of the report. Cite all references that you have footnoted in your report and all other references that were of assistance to you in the research. You are not obligated to include every book, periodical, or article you reviewed. Include only those that were useful to you. Keep in mind, though, that some topics may permit you to make a contribution by summarizing, or listing, all the pertinent reference works on the topic.

The appendices will depend entirely upon your particular

topic. Use an appendix when the continuity of your writing might be interrupted if the material were included in the text. This technique is another indication of an organized writer, one who tries to keep the flow of his written material uninterrupted by data that can be conveniently placed in an appendix.

Another possible approach to the table of contents is the following descriptive table of contents.*

Chapter 1 GENERAL INTRODUCTION
      a. Statement of objectives
      b. Definition of key terms
      c. General background information
      d. Limitations of the study
      e. Nature and order of presentation

Chapter 2 REVIEW OF EXISTING LITERATURE
      a. Summary of the different points of view on the subject matter as found in books, periodicals, and articles
      b. Critical evaluation of these views, indicating strengths and weaknesses of the literature
      c. General conclusions about the state of the art at the time of writing

Chapter 3 CONCEPTUAL FRAMEWORK AND METHODOLOGY
      a. Statement of hypotheses
      b. Discussion of the research methodology used; relationship between hypotheses and objectives of the study
      c. Discussion of the sources and means of obtaining data (special emphasis should be placed upon the limitations and conclusions generated by the methodology used)

Chapter 4 ANALYSIS OF THE DATA (one to three chapters)
      a. Testing of the hypothesis or hypotheses, using the data collected. At the end of each chapter in this part of the dissertation, it might be useful to develop key conclusions concerning the problems analyzed in the chapter. A summary should be prepared for each chapter.

* I wish to thank G. Peter Lauter for bringing this descriptive table of contents to my attention.

Chapter 5 GENERAL CONCLUSIONS (last chapter)
   a. Restatement of objectives
   b. Conclusions with respect to support or rejection of the hypothesis or hypotheses
   c. Conclusions with respect to stated objectives of the study
   d. Suggested areas for further research
   e. Discussion of possible implication of the study for a model, group, theory, discipline

BIBLIOGRAPHY AND APPENDICES
   (as described in the manual for dissertations at your school)

As the two tables of contents presented here suggest, there is a pattern to the organization of the research report for academic research. No one approach is better than any other, but the pattern is to present the statement of purpose in the early part of the paper, conduct the analysis and interpretation in the middle section, and present a summary and conclusions as the final part of the paper.

Review the table of contents of dissertations and theses similar to your topic that have been approved at your school. They may provide you with a method for organizing your own thoughts.

How long should the dissertation be?

Many students worry about how long the dissertation should be when they should be concerned with the quality of the report. There appears to be a favorable and much-needed trend toward brief, concise dissertations. (What is your school's policy on this matter?) In any event, there is certainly no necessary relationship between the quality of a dissertation and its length, unless one could say that the briefer the dissertation, the more apt it is to reflect sharp and clear thinking.

Do not pad your final report. Take enough pages to do your topic justice and to cover the material well. If you really need some firm guidelines about length, the rule of thumb often used is from one hundred to three hundred pages. Check with your research chairman on his idea of a "ballpark" figure and look at the length of dissertations approved at your school. But in general tend toward brevity. Professors will appreciate it.

Is it better to submit the draft of the final report all at once or one chapter at a time?

The approach that you use will depend upon the desires of your committee (especially the chairman); however, there are several guidelines that can assist you in determining which approach you should favor.

If you write the research report as a total unit (instead of chapter by chapter), you can more easily produce cohesion and uniformity in the total paper. Also, you can write the part of the paper that is easiest or most interesting to you at the moment—a big item if writing is not your strong point. (Often the beginning of the paper is the hardest part to write; in fact, a good case could be made for writing the first chapter last.) You will be able to see interrelationships among chapters if you keep the whole report in front of you, and you can write parts of the paper that are similar in structure or approach all at once. The total writing task will seem smaller than it is, as you write small segments and continue to build a sizable volume.

Writing and submitting one chapter at a time also has its advantages. It allows you to correct your writing faults (should you have any) in the early stages of your writing. It may also give you a sense of accomplishment as you complete each chapter before going on to the next one. This approach may be consistent with your style or method of writing. Or the type of dissertation may be such that each chapter is relatively independent of previous and subsequent chapters.

Submitting one chapter at a time has two distinct disadvantages: the paper may become disjointed and lack any sense of cohesion; and you may have to write the chapters in sequence, which may not be the most advantageous way to write the paper.

Discuss both approaches to writing with your research committee chairman. If he is not strongly committed to one particular approach, you might try to sell him on the unit approach. It should save time for members of the committee and should result in a report that is well organized and presented.

Can you suggest a few writing hints and shortcuts that I could use?

1. Allot large segments of time to writing—anywhere from two to eight hours per day, or for days at a time if you can arrange it. But take a break when your mind feels cluttered or bogged down. Do something physical like bowling, swimming, golfing, or tennis.

2. Keep the table of contents handy, and refer to it often. You will probably modify the table of contents as you get into the final writing. This is to be expected, as new patterns and relationships emerge. Whenever you change the organization, retype the new table of contents and refer to it constantly. Constant reference to the table of contents should give you the perspective of always knowing how your writing fits into the total report. Maintain this perspective.

3. Do not become sidetracked by taking a part of the report and trying to produce an article for publication. Keep in mind that the task at hand is completion. There will be plenty of time to publish your research. Don't jeopardize getting finished or extending the writing time by diverting your effort to potential articles. The possible gain is not worth the probable loss of time and continuity. Finish the writing.

4. If you were teaching while completing the program, try to reduce your teaching load. Or teach courses that you have already taught, so that your preparation time will be minimized. Don't experiment with new courses while writing the dissertation. Pour your creativity and energy into your writing.

5. Try to arrange your schedule so that your most productive time is free for writing. If you like to write in the early hours of the morning, and you must teach while you are writing, try to arrange

your classes for the evening. Or if you like to write late in the evening, try to teach afternoon or early-evening classes.

6. Reduce or eliminate outside activities until the report is finished. At least cut down on nonessential activities until the first draft has been placed in the hands of your chairman.

7. If you are working full time and completing the dissertation on a part-time basis, try to reduce your workload while writing the report. If possible, use vacation time to start or to complete your writing. Try not to accept new responsibilities or a new job while you are writing the dissertation. The longer you take in the writing process, the less your chances of completion.

8. Use a three-ring binder to "build" the completed draft. Place index tabs for each chapter, and insert draft material as it is completed. Build the dissertation a section at a time. Do not, however, look at the draft as having a preconceived and inflexible format. Expect to make changes as you go along.

9. Check the footnote and bibliographical references to ensure that you have all required information for each footnote and reference. (You should have done this long in advance of the writing, perhaps when you were collecting the references.) Number your footnotes by page, regardless of the required format. During the final draft the footnotes can be renumbered if required. This procedure will eliminate the problem of renumbering footnotes should you make changes in your draft or your table of contents.

10. Use your proposal for the first three chapters, or wherever else you can use it. If the proposal is written properly, the essence of the first three chapters could be written for you.

11. Begin each section on a separate page for your first draft. Don't try to save a few pages. It is easier to expand and make changes when each section starts on a fresh page. You will be able to add or delete entire sections with less retyping.

12. If you are making only one copy of your draft, do something to protect yourself against loss by fire or some other misfortune. At various stages in the drafting, for instance, you might reproduce what you have written to date and put the material in

some safe place remote from the original draft. The availability of relatively inexpensive reproduction equipment makes this concept (called "the concept of freeze points") practical. If your data is on punched cards, these cards also can be reproduced and placed in a safe location.

13. When you have finished a chapter, or a large section of a chapter, ask your research committee chairman to evaluate your writing style. Find out what faults you might have before you are too far into the writing of the draft.

14. If you type, consider drafting the report on the typewriter. From loose outlines of the various sections, you may be able to capture the essence of your material while composing on the typewriter. Or, if you are familiar with dictating equipment, consider using it to get the major parts of the first draft on paper. Use that method which will allow you to get your material on paper quickly.

15. When you have the draft ready for the committee, check with the research chairman to see if you can prepare separate copies for each member of the committee. This will save time, since the members will not have to pass one copy among themselves.

What manual of format and style should I use for my research project?

Find out which one is required at your school, and use this style for every research paper you have to write or for every term paper. This will give you sufficient time to become very familiar with that manual. It is questionable, however, whether you should know in complete detail any particular style for research reports. Check with the graduate office to locate a typist who has experience with the style required at your school, and get that typist to type your final report. Learn those aspects of the style that you need to know (such as what material is contained in a footnote or bibliographical entry) with the least investment of your time. But concentrate your efforts on the *content* of the research report; let the typist handle format and style.

What items should be in my bibliography?

Some topics suggest a literature research that is almost un-manageable. With the proliferation of published material, the wise doctoral candidate avoids topics that present special problems with the literature. The problem can be minimized by concentrating on *relevant* literature, and being highly selective about what is relevant.

You should discuss the literature with your chairman and attempt to establish a cutoff period for the literature search. For example, the past five years of literature would be sufficient, since the field of study has probably changed enough in that period to cast doubts on material (except classics) researched prior to the five-year period. Also, as the defense approaches, set a cutoff time for current material that can influence the final written report. For example, if the defense is scheduled in April, you and the research chairman may agree that any material published after February 1 will not be reflected in the report. Of course, if significant findings occur, and you want to put these in the report, you should make every effort to do so. And you should be current on the literature in preparation for the defense (discussed further in Chapter Seven). Try to reach an agreement with your research committee chairman on the scope of the literature search, the time period covered, and the cutoff date for current literature to include in the final bibliography. These actions could save you and the committee much time and effort.

On what basis will my dissertation be reviewed and evaluated?

Dissertations and theses must be reviewed and approved before the student has completed the requirements of his program. It is important to know what the person who is reviewing your paper thinks are the critical components of an effective research effort.

Knowing these criteria will assist you in preparing your final report. This following list* contains some of the criteria that a reviewer might use in evaluating a thesis or dissertation. The material is illustrative only. It is offered as a guide and perhaps a warning of potential problems.

Read this list before you begin your writing. Review it from time to time. Try to determine the specific criteria upon which your work will be judged. Remember that it is far easier to incorporate items into the final report as you are writing it than to make the insertions after your draft is completed.

SAMPLE GUIDE TO THESIS REVIEW

A. Introductory Chapters

1. Was the problem *area* defined?

2. Was research and writing relevant to the problem area (a) well covered, (b) accurately described, (c) demonstrated as relevant to the problem?

3. Was the research or thesis question handled well?
    (a) Was its relevance to the problem area stated?
    (b) Were the questions and subsidiary questions clearly stated?
    (c) Was the scope of the questions clearly defined?

4. Was the intended approach of the study clearly defined?
    (a) Was the methodology briefly stated?

* This list is made available to each graduate student in the School of Government and Business Administration at George Washington University and was developed by members of that faculty.

(b) Were hypotheses as derived from the research questions set forth?

(c) Were definitions presented where needed?

5. Were the statements of the problem, the question, and the approach logical and internally consistent?

6. Were alternative solutions or approaches briefly suggested and discussed? Was their exclusion from the thesis justified?

B. Methodology Chapters

1. Did the methodology description follow a logical sequence?

2. Were steps clearly delineated?

3. Were relationships of methodology to the research questions clearly demonstrated?

4. Were controls in the research adequately handled?

5. Were assumptions about uncontrollable factors stated?

6. Were appropriate materials appendixed?

C. Results Chapters

1. Was the success of the data collection discussed?

2. Were the appropriate analytical methods chosen and described?

3. Were the results clearly presented?

(a) Were tables neat, logical, and self-explanatory?

(b) Did discussions of tables include not merely descriptions of results but also interpretations?

4. Were hypotheses restated (or research questions) to ease the reader's burden?

5. Were adequate statements made regarding the support or rejection of hypotheses?

6. Was the sequence of presentation of results in consonance with the sequence of research questions and/or hypotheses?

7. Were appropriate data, tables, charts appendixed?

D. Discussion and Conclusion Chapters

1. Were the thoughts presented in a logical sequence, also consonant with the preceding chapters? Were references to tables made?

2. Were discussions logical, critical, analytical?

3. Were alternative explanations for the results offered?

4. Were conclusions within the limits of the results obtained; were they sound and based upon the body of the thesis?

5. Were recommendations (if at all necessary) soundly derived from the results and conclusions? Were limitations delineated?

6. Was the contribution to the field (or the problem area) defined adequately?

E. Overall Thesis Questions

1. Was the title relevant, descriptive, adequate?

2. Did the table of contents reflect the most logical method for organizing the report?

3. Were all areas of the thesis well handled?

4. Was the bibliography adequate, up to date, complete but not padded?

5. Were tables and appendixes in the order referred to in the body of the thesis? Were all appendixes referred to in the body of the thesis?

What is an abstract?

An abstract is a condensation of the final report. It should contain the purpose of the study, the hypotheses or research questions that were addressed, the scope and method of the study, a brief summary of the conclusions related to the hypotheses or research questions, and implications of the research for those who might wish to read the completed report. An abstract permits an interested reader to determine whether he would like to read the full report.

The length of the abstract will vary by school. Normally, an abstract will be five hundred to seven hundred words, or from two to three typed pages. Often abstracts are prepared for distribution prior to the oral defense of the dissertation. You should be able to get copies of abstracts from dissertations that have been completed at your school to use as samples.

THE FOLLOWING QUESTIONS, RELATED TO YOUR SCHOOL AND INTERESTS, ARE PRESENTED TO GUIDE YOUR THINKING TOWARD THE SUCCESSFUL WRITING OF THE REPORT.

1. What is the average length of dissertations and theses at your school? More specifically, what is the average length for your type of dissertation?

2. What is the approved writing format at your school?

3. What approach is favored for writing the report, a chapter at a time or all at once? What does your potential research committee chairman think is the best method?

4. How long are dissertation and thesis abstracts?

5. Is there clerical assistance provided to master's or doctoral students who are at the writing stage in their research?

6. Are reproduction facilities available to master's or doctoral students? What is the cost?

7. Is financial support available to defray part of the writing costs?

8. What criteria are used to judge the completed thesis or dissertation? What are the thoughts of your research committee chairman?

9. How much time is normally expected for the actual writing of a thesis or dissertation?

10. Are there any guidelines for format and table of contents for theses and dissertations? Is the generalized format discussed in this chapter acceptable for your topic at your school?

SEVEN

Dissertation Defense

The final stage in the dissertation process is the dissertation defense, more commonly called the oral defense. The primary purpose of the defense is to have the candidate demonstrate his ability to support and justify his research methodology, findings, and interpretations. Another purpose is to determine whether the candidate has in fact completed all aspects of the dissertation himself. No doctoral candidate should consider any alternative other than to complete all aspects of the work on his own initiative. A doctoral candidate who would attempt to enter the defense with research conducted by someone other than himself should not be permitted to complete his studies.

The candidate should enter the defense fully prepared to answer searching questions on all phases of his research. Normally, no serious student should have any difficulty with the defense if he has taken the steps outlined in various parts of this book. The defense should be clearly kept in mind from the first stages of the dissertation preparation. Questions likely to occur in the defense should be properly answered in the dissertation. Since the dissertation is a

research effort that must be defended, the candidate should incorporate ironclad defensible parts into his final report.

Who conducts the dissertation defense, and how is it conducted?

The candidate's research committee, often augmented by
two or three other faculty members, usually conducts the defense.
Often a "non-academic" person with related or additional expertise
in the topic area is invited to participate as a member of the defense
committee.

The chairman of the research committee often serves as
chairman and starts the defense by asking the candidate some introductory questions—for instance, "What have you accomplished in
your research?" or "Would you briefly summarize your entire research effort?" The candidate should discuss the opening of the
defense with his chairman prior to the defense. Since the approach
may vary with the school or the faculty members involved, it is
important for the candidate to find out what he can expect at the
beginning of the defense.

The best way to find out how dissertation defenses are conducted at your school is to *attend one or more defenses*. The defense
often is open to the public, and doctoral candidates are encouraged
to attend. If you are not allowed to attend the defense at your
school, perhaps a nearby school has an "open defense" policy. If
you cannot attend any defense, at least talk to someone who has
recently successfully defended his work at your school.

The pattern followed in the defense is much the same from
university to university, or between schools in the same university.
Once the defense is underway, members of the committee begin
asking questions. Each member of the defense committee is allotted
a certain amount of time (variable) to ask any question he deems
appropriate. Other members of the committee may "hitchhike" on
questions in advance of their turn to question the candidate. But
the questioning normally follows an organized pattern from the
chairman of the research committee to the other members.

Once the questioning is completed (which may be from a half hour to five or six hours—figure on two hours), the candidate is normally excused from the room. Then the committee deliberates and decides whether the candidate has successfully defended and whether the dissertation as presented is acceptable. Small changes often have to be made. Suggestions for changes are normally turned over to the chairman of the research committee, and he ensures that they are incorporated into the dissertation by the candidate. If major changes are required, the entire research committee might have to review the dissertation after the changes are incorporated. Obviously, it is very desirable to keep the number and type of changes to a minimum. Careful planning and effort prior to the defense should minimize the number of changes to be made.

How can I prepare for the dissertation defense?

Once you have found out what to expect in the defense, it is a relatively easy matter to prepare yourself. Find out what kinds of questions you can anticipate from members of the research or defense committee. Find out also how your research fits in with other research related to the topic. See what appears in current journals on the topic. Remember that the time from your proposal to the time of your defense may be several months or even years. Much could have happened during this time which you could not incorporate into the dissertation, but you could be expected to respond to such questions in the dissertation defense. (This *time lag* further emphasizes the importance of speeding up your dissertation.) Scan the current journals in your field from the time of your proposal to the time of your defense, and be particularly aware of the current month's journal in your field. Defense committee members often like to ask a question from the preceding day's local newspaper or from the current issue of a related journal to see whether the candidate is on top of his subject.

Often members of the committee will have published material relevant to your research. It is a prudent investment of time to keep abreast of the thinking of the members of your defense committee. A recent publication of a member of your committee that is unknown to you might make for an embarrassing moment in the defense. Prepare for such a situation and avoid the embarrassment.

Even though you have spent considerable time on all phases of the dissertation, it would be a good idea to read the entire paper from beginning to end just prior to the defense. Try to step back from your material and pretend that your are one of the committee members reading it for the first time. Try to anticipate what questions might be asked. Formulate your answers and perhaps verbalize them. You might even ask a friend to read the dissertation and develop a list of questions that come to mind. Then attempt to answer them for him.

Can I bring a copy of my dissertation to the defense?

In many schools the candidate is allowed to bring a copy of his paper into the defense and to refer to it freely. What is the policy of your school in this matter? How does your committee chairman feel about it?

In some schools the candidate is also permitted to prepare a brief presentation—using slides, flip charts, handouts—and to make this presentation at the beginning of the defense. What is the policy of your school on this approach to the defense? What does your committee chairman want?

It would probably be wise to prepare a summary presentation even though you may not be asked to bring it to the defense. You still might be asked to summarize your research efforts and conclusions. Your answer can be much more effective if you have prepared in advance for the question.

What kinds of questions should I expect in the defense?

Of course, the nature of your topic will dictate the kinds of questions asked. Here I will assume that you are able to handle questions related to the substance of your paper, and list other kinds of questions that you might expect. (By attending one or two defenses, you will see a pattern of questioning emerge.) (1) "A dissertation is supposed to be a contribution to the literature. What is your contribution?" (2) "Who, in your area of study, would agree with your findings? Why? Who would disagree? Why?" (3) "What are the major strengths and weaknesses of your study?" (4) "What questions were you unable to answer with your research?" (5) "What areas for further research did you uncover?" (6) "How did you reduce your biases and prejudices?" (7) "What additional work do you intend to undertake as a result of your study?" (8) "Where could you publish your findings to reach the audience that could profit most from your work?" (9) "What did this exercise in research teach you?" (10) "How do you intend to use your findings?"

Since the defense is the final examination in the doctoral program, the candidate should also be prepared to respond to questions that may be only remotely related to his dissertation. In some schools, the defense is strictly confined to the research work, since another set of examinations has already been passed by the candidate. It is important to know exactly what questions are appropriate for the defense at your school.

How should I handle questions at the defense?

Your role in the defense is to answer searching questions regarding your research. You will not know the answers to all questions. If you don't know, say "I don't know." Don't try to bluff your way in a defense. The committee will expect you to be asked questions that you cannot answer. You will only lose if you try to pretend that you know when in fact you don't.

Formulate sharp, concise, and accurate answers when such answers are appropriate. Answer the question first, then elaborate more if needed. Don't ramble, but don't be too brief either. After an answer, you might say: "Does that answer your question, Dr. Allen?" or "Would you like me to elaborate?"

Don't lose your poise in the defense. Some member of the defense committee may intentionally try to irritate you. Don't let yourself get irritated. You can't think straight when you are upset, so keep as calm as you can. Practice patience and constraint.

When you are asked for your opinion, and you have an opinion, express yourself. At this point in your doctoral program, you should have formulated some opinions of your own. Don't be afraid to voice them, even if you think that members of the committee differ with you. Simply preface your remarks by clearly indicating that these are your opinions. If you have no opinion on a particular question asked, simply answer that you have no opinion formulated at this time. If pressed, however, you probably should give an opinion.

Some members of the defense committee will be disappointed if you don't respond at least once by saying: "I don't know." They remember when they had to make the same statement at their own defense. They may even be intentionally trying to get you to say "I don't know." Be prepared, and say it when you mean it.

What should I do if I don't understand a question?

Expect to be asked questions that are not completely clear. When a question is asked that you do not completely understand, ask that the question be rephrased or restated. Be sure you know what you are being asked to respond to. Also, if you are a little uncertain about an answer, having the question rephrased will give you a little more time to formulate an answer. It is better to spend additional time having the question restated than to answer the wrong question. You may even rephrase the question yourself and ask whether you are stating it properly. Sharp, precise answers to clearly stated questions make for an effective dissertation defense.

What happens when the questioning session is completed?

When the questioning session is over, you may be asked to say a few words. If you are given this opportunity, thank the committee members for their patience and indulgence during the defense, and thank the members of your research committee for their efforts on your behalf during the entire research project. Don't exaggerate or belabor the point. Just remember that you would not be at the defense if it had not been for your committee.

How is the voting conducted in the dissertation defense? Must all members of the committee approve the dissertation?

The voting procedures vary widely among schools and universities. At some schools, all members must approve the dissertation; at others, one dissenting vote is allowed; at still others, only a majority vote for approval is needed. What is the procedure at your school?

The student may be asked to leave the room when the committee is deliberating in preparation for the vote. After the vote is taken, the candidate is then asked to return to the room for the decision. Usually, minor changes are required, and these are often left to the discretion of the chairman to see that they are incorporated into the paper. If you have conscientiously applied the material in this book, and have listened to the advice of your committee, and have fully prepared for the defense, then you need never consider the possibility of doing anything except passing the dissertation defense, regardless of the method used in the voting.

THE FOLLOWING QUESTIONS, RELATED TO YOUR SCHOOL, SHOULD ASSIST YOU IN PREPARING FOR THE DISSERTATION DEFENSE.

1. Does the research committee chairman think that you are ready for the defense?

2. Do you think that you are ready for the defense?

3. Do all members of your committee think that you are ready?

4. Does your school permit you to attend oral defenses?

5. Are there any nearby schools that permit you to attend a defense?

6. How is the defense conducted at your school?

7. How many members are on the defense committee?

8. Have you any influence over the selection of the committee?

9. How is the voting conducted? How many members must vote to ensure that a candidate passes his defense?

10. Are you up to date on current journals in your field?

11. Are you permitted to bring a copy of your dissertation to the defense? Can you refer to it freely?

12. Are you permitted to present a brief summary of your study and findings to open the defense? How long should this be?

13. What is the philosophy of your school on the types of questions that can occur in the defense? Are the questions restricted to the dissertation topic, or can they cover any aspect of your program of study?

Questions Answered
in the Text

CHAPTER 1. ACADEMIC RESEARCH

What is the purpose of a doctoral dissertation? (1)

A dissertation is supposed to be a "contribution to knowledge." What is a contribution to knowledge? (2)

Do different fields (such as the social sciences and the physical sciences) have different requirements for an acceptable dissertation or thesis? (3)

Why should I worry about the dissertation process now, since my comprehensives are about two years away? (3)

Can I afford to waste any of my scarce time working on the dissertation when I first have to complete my courses and comprehensives? (4)

Since I am going to make a large investment in time on the dissertation, why not write a paper than can be published? (5)

How much time should it take to complete a dissertation? (5)

Why should I be in a hurry to complete my research? (6)

I have a great job offer that I will lose if I don't accept it now. What difference will it make if I complete the dissertation while I am working at my job? (7)

Are there any particular problems that I might encounter in trying to get such financial assistance (a grant or other funding) for my research? (8)

Can you suggest some ways that I could reduce the cost of my research? (9)

CHAPTER 2. SELECTING THE RESEARCH TOPIC

What are the characteristics of a potential topic? (12)

How interested should I be in the dissertation topic? (13)

Some members of the faculty think that I have a potential topic for a dissertation; others think it has no potential whatsoever. Why such a wide divergence of viewpoints in the same faculty? (13)

How strongly should I try to sell the merits of my topic? (14)

When should I start looking for a dissertation topic? (14)

My school has a rule that we are not permitted even to talk about our research projects before the comprehensives are completed, let alone begin any part of the process. What do I do? (15)

I am preparing for the comprehensives. Why should I be bothered with looking for dissertation topics? (15)

Questions Answered in the Text

I just reviewed several dissertations that were approved at my school and was surprised. They did not seem like dissertations to me. How could they have been approved and defended? (16)

What are the advantages and disadvantages of using term papers as springboards to theses or dissertations? (16)

What are some other possible sources of potential topics? (18)

In checking the dissertation abstracts to see whether others have written on a topic I am considering, how many years back should I go? (21)

Checklist for Evaluating Potential Research Topics. (22–26)

CHAPTER 3. RESEARCH COMMITTEE

What is the role of the research committee chairman? (29)

Will I be allowed to select my research committee? If so, whom should I try to get on the committee? (30)

Who has to approve my research proposal—the entire committee or only the chairman? (31)

CHAPTER 4. RESEARCH PROPOSAL

What benefits should I expect from a well-prepared research proposal? (34)

What should I include in my research proposal? (35)

Sample Proposal Format. (36–37)

Must the research proposal be defended? (38)

If I have successfully defended my dissertation proposal, do I have a contract with the school that my topic is acceptable for a dissertation? (38)

Should my hypotheses or research questions be spelled out in the proposal, or could they be put in final form after the proposal is completed? (39)

Is it permissible for me to deviate from my original proposal while I am conducting my research? (40)

If I do deviate slightly from my original proposal, must I revise it and get approval of the changes? (40)

How do I get a proposal prepared and approved? (41)

CHAPTER 5. DATA COLLECTION AND ANALYSIS

How can I be sure that the data I collect are directly related to my hypotheses or research questions? (44)

I know plenty of doctoral candidates with mountains of data, but they can't seem to complete their dissertations. Why? (44)

What happens if I do not support my hypotheses or research questions? Will I have to start my dissertation over again? (45)

How can I eliminate my biases in data collection and analysis? (45)

What is the difference between interpretation *and* analysis *of data? (46)*

Do I have to use statistical tests to analyze my data? (47)

If I use statistical tests for analyzing my data, won't I have to defend my choice of tests? (48)

Can I use a computer in my research when I have only limited knowledge about computers? (48)

I want to learn about computers. How can I learn about them quickly? (50)

Can I use already published data instead of generating the data myself? (51)

Can a questionnaire or an interview be used to collect data for a dissertation or thesis? (51)

How can I construct an effective questionnaire? (52)

Where can I find people to complete my questionnaire or to provide data in some other form? (56)

I plan to administer a questionnaire to a group (or several groups) of respondents. How can I conceal their identity so that they will feel free to give me reliable and truthful data? (57)

If I am collecting data from questionnaires or interviews, how do I know whether the people are telling the truth or merely what they think I want to hear? (58)

I will be using a mailing procedure to collect my data. What are the advantages of this procedure? What problems should I anticipate? (59)

What is an acceptable return rate for a mailing? How can I increase this return rate? (60)

CHAPTER 6. WRITING THE RESEARCH REPORT

Is there any general pattern of organization for research papers? (65)

General Format for a Table of Contents. (65–66)

Descriptive Table of Contents. (70–71)

How long should the dissertation be? (71)

CHAPTER 7. DISSERTATION DEFENSE

Bibliography

Books

BARBER, R. J. *The Politics of Research*. Washington, D.C.: Public Affairs Press, 1966.

BARZUN, J. M. *The Modern Researcher*. New York: Harcourt Brace Jovanovich, 1970.

BERELSON, C., AND COLTON, R. *Research and Report Writing for Business and Economics*. New York: Random House, 1971.

BEVERIDGE, W. I. B. *The Art of Scientific Investigation*. New York: Random House, 1957.

BLALOCK, H. M. *Theory Construction; From Verbal to Mathematical Formulation*. Englewood Cliffs, N.J.: Prentice-Hall, 1969.

BLALOCK, H. M. *An Introduction to Social Research*. Englewood Cliffs, N.J.: Prentice-Hall, 1970.

BROOKS, P. C. *Research in Archives; The Use of Unpublished Primary Sources*. Chicago: University of Chicago Press, 1969.

97

Bibliography

BROWN, A. F. *Statistical Physics*. New York: American Elsevier, 1968.

BUTLER, J. M., RICE, L. N., AND WAGSTAFF, A. K. *Quantitative Naturalistic Research*. Englewood Cliffs, N.J.: Prentice-Hall, 1963.

CAMPBELL, W. G. *Form and Style in Thesis Writing*. Boston: Houghton Mifflin, 1969. One of the most widely accepted manuals addressing style and format for academic research. Required format at some institutions.

COHEN, N. M. *Library Science Dissertations: 1925–1960 (An Annotated Bibliography of Doctoral Studies)*. Washington, D.C.: Government Printing Office, 1963.

DICKSON, P. *Think Tanks*. New York: Atheneum, 1971.

DOWNS, R. B. *How To Do Library Research*. Urbana: University of Illinois Press, 1966.

EILENBERG, H. *What You Should Know About Research Techniques for Retailers*. Dobbs Ferry, N.Y.: Oceana, 1968.

ERDOS, P. L., AND MORGAN, A. J. *Professional Mail Surveys*. New York: McGraw-Hill, 1970. A useful reference if you are using the mails for your research. Should help increase your returns.

FERBER, R., AND VERDOORN, P. J. *Research Methods in Economics and Business*. New York: Macmillan, 1962. A widely used text in the area of economics and business.

FISHLOCK, D. *The New Scientists*. New York: Oxford University Press, 1971.

FLOOD, K. U. *Research in Transportation*. Detroit: Gale Research, 1970.

FREEMAN, H. E. *Social Research and Social Policy*. Englewood Cliffs, N.J.: Prentice-Hall, 1970.

FREUND, J. E. *Statistics; A First Course*. Englewood Cliffs, N.J.: Prentice-Hall, 1972.

FREUND, J. E., AND WILLIAMS, F. J. *Elementary Business Statistics; The Modern Approach*. Englewood Cliffs, N.J.: Prentice-Hall, 1972.

Bibliography

GATNER, E. S., AND CORDASCO, F. *Research and Report Writing*. New York: Barnes and Noble, 1961.

GOOD, C. V. *Introduction to Educational Research*. New York: Appleton-Century-Crofts, 1963. If you are conducting research in the area of education, this is an excellent book to use.

GOOD, C. V., AND SCATES, D. E. *Methods of Research: Educational, Psychological, and Sociological*. New York: Appleton-Century-Crofts, 1954.

GREER, S. A. *The Logic of Social Inquiry*. Chicago: Aldine-Atherton, 1969.

GUETZKOW, H. S., AND OTHERS. *Simulation in Social and Administrative Science*. Englewood Cliffs, N.J.: Prentice-Hall, 1972.

HALO, R. P. *A Directory of Governmental, Public and Urban Affairs Research Centers in the United States*. Berkeley: University of California Institute of Governmental Studies, 1969.

HEERMAN, E. F., AND BRASKAMP, L. A. *Readings in Statistics for the Behavioral Sciences*. Englewood Cliffs, N.J.: Prentice-Hall, 1970.

HILLWAY, T. *Introduction to Research*. Boston: Houghton Mifflin, 1964.

HOOK, L. *The Research Paper*. Englewood Cliffs, N.J.: Prentice-Hall, 1969.

ISARD, W. *Methods of Regional Analysis*. Cambridge, Mass.: M.I.T. Press, 1960.

JOHN, P. W. M. *Statistical Design and Analysis of Experiments*. New York: Macmillan, 1971.

JOHNSON, H. W. *How to Use the Business Library, with Sources of Business Information*. Cincinnati: South-Western, 1972.

KALVELAGE, C., SEGAL, M., AND ANDERSON, P. J. *Research Guide for Undergraduates in Political Science*. Morristown N.J.: General Learning Corporation, 1972.

KAZMIER, L. J. *Statistical Analysis for Business and Economics*. New York: McGraw-Hill, 1967. A readable programed-instruction approach to statistics.

99

Bibliography

KING, L. J. *Statistical Analysis in Geography*. Englewood Cliffs, N.J.: Prentice-Hall, 1969.

KLEIN, R. M., AND KLEIN, D. T. *Research Methods in Plant Science*. Garden City, N.Y.: Doubleday, 1970.

LABOVITZ, S., AND HAGEDON, R. *Introduction to Social Research*. New York: McGraw-Hill, 1972.

LODGE, A. *A Guide to Research Materials for Graduate Students*. Berkeley: University of California Press, 1964.

MC LEAN, J. *Statistical Sources; A Subject Guide to Data on Industrial, Business, Social, Educational, Financial, and Other Topics for the United States and Selected Foreign Countries*. Detroit: Gale Research, 1971. This text is helpful if you are considering research based upon existing statistical data.

MC NAMEE, L. F. *Dissertations in English and American Literature (Theses Accepted by American, British and German Universities, 1865–1964)*. New York: Bowker, 1968.

MERRITT, R. L., AND PYSZKA, G. J. *The Student Political Scientist's Handbook*. Cambridge, Mass.: Schenkman, 1969.

MILLER, D. C. *Handbook of Research Design and Social Measurement*. New York: McKay, 1970.

MILLER, R. B. *Statistical Concepts and Applications; A Nonmathematical Explanation*. Chicago: Science Research Associates, 1968.

MORSE, G. W. *The Concise Guide to Library Research*. New York: Washington Square Press, 1966. You might want to use this text if you are involved in library research.

NOLTINGK, B. *The Art of Research: A Guide for the Graduate*. New York: American Elsevier, 1965.

PHILLIPS, B. S. *Social Research; Strategy and Tactics*. New York: Macmillan, 1971.

PREHODA, R. W. *Designing the Future: The Role of Technological Forecasting*. Philadelphia: Chilton, 1967.

PUGH, G. T. *Guide to Research Writing*. Boston: Houghton Mifflin, 1963.

Bibliography

RIEBEL, J. P. *How to Write Reports, Papers, Theses, and Articles.* New York: Arco, 1972.

RIGBY, P. H. *Conceptual Foundations of Business Research.* New York: Wiley, 1965.

RUMMEL, F. J., AND BALLAINE, W. C. *Research Methodology in Business.* New York: Harper and Row, 1963.

SEEBER, E. D. *A Style Manual for Students: For the Preparation of Term Papers, Essays and Theses.* Bloomington: Indiana University Press, 1967.

SELYE, H. *From Dream to Discovery; On Being a Scientist.* New York: McGraw-Hill, 1964.

SHULMAN, F. J. *Japan and Korea; An Annotated Bibliography of Doctoral Dissertations in Western Languages—1877–1969.* Chicago: American Library Association, 1970. Check this source if your research involves Western languages.

SIEGEL, S. *Non-Parametric Statistics.* New York: McGraw-Hill, 1956. Highly recommended as a reference text in the area of nonparametric statistics.

SJOBERG, G., AND NETT, R. *A Methodology for Social Research.* New York: Harper and Row, 1968.

SMITH, L. H., AND WILLIAMS, D. R. *Statistical Analysis for Business: A Conceptual Approach.* Belmont, Calif.: Wadsworth, 1971.

STEVENS, R. E. *Research Methods in Librarianship.* Champaign: University of Illinois Graduate School of Library Science, 1971.

STONE, P. J. *The General Inquirer; A Computer Approach to Content Analysis.* Cambridge, Mass.: M.I.T. Press, 1966.

SUCHMAN, E. A. *Evaluative Research; Principles and Practices in Public Service and Social Action Programs.* New York: Russell Sage Foundation, 1967.

TAYLOR, E. B. *Researches into the Early History of Mankind and the Development of Civilization.* Edited and abridged by P. Bohannan. Chicago: University of Chicago Press, 1964.

101

Bibliography

TAYLOR, M. *Basic Reference Sources*. Metuchen, N.J.: Scarecrow, 1971.

THOMLINSON, R. *Sociological Concepts and Research*. New York: Random House, 1965.

TOY, H. *Federal Dollars for Scholars*. Washington, D.C.: Nu-Toy, 1970.

TURABIAN, K. L. *A Manual for Writers of Term Papers, Theses, and Dissertations*. Chicago: University of Chicago Press, 1967. One of the most widely used manuals concerning style and format. A required manual at many institutions.

TURABIAN, K. L. *A Students' Guide for Writing College Papers*. Chicago: University of Chicago Press, 1969.

WASSON, C. R. *Understanding Quantitative Analysis*. New York: Appleton-Century-Crofts, 1969.

WIRT, F. M. *Introductory Problems in Political Research*. Englewood Cliffs, N.J.: Prentice-Hall, 1970.

WYNAR, B. S. *Research Methods in Library Science: A Bibliographical Guide with Topical Outlines*. Littleton, Colo.: Libraries Unlimited, 1971.

YOUNG, H. D. *Statistical Treatment of Experimental Data*. New York: McGraw-Hill, 1962.

ZUCKERMAN, S. *Beyond the Ivory Tower; The Frontiers of Public and Private Science*. New York: Taplinger, 1970.

Periodical Indexes

Agricultural Index. New York: H. W. Wilson, since 1906.

Education Index. New York: H. W. Wilson, since 1929.

Index to Legal Periodicals. New York: H. W. Wilson, since 1908.

International Index to Periodical Literature. New York: H. W. Wilson, since 1907.

Poole's Index to Periodical Literature. Boston: Houghton Mifflin, 1892 to 1906.

The Public Affairs Information Service. New York, since 1915.

Bibliography

Reader's Guide to Periodical Literature. New York: H. W. Wilson, since 1900.

Bibliographies

Books in Print. New York: Bowker.

The Cumulative Book Index. New York: H. W. Wilson, for the United States since 1898; for other English-speaking countries since 1928.

The Publishers Trade List Annual. New York: Bowker.

Subject Guide to Books in Print. New York: Bowker.

United States Catalogue. New York: H. W. Wilson, 1899 to 1934.

Abstracts

BUROS, O. K. (Ed.) *Research in Statistical Methodology, Books and Reviews, 1933–1938.* 2 Vols. New Brunswick, N.J.: Rutgers University Press, 1938.

BUROS, O. K. (Ed.) *Statistical Methodology Reviews, 1941–1950.* New York: Wiley, 1951.

Dissertation Abstracts International. Ann Arbor, Mich.: University Microfilms.

Psychological Abstracts. Lancaster, Pa.: American Psychological Association, since 1927.

Social Science Abstracts. New York: Social Science Abstracts, Columbia University, 1929 to 1932.

Sociological Abstracts. New York: Social Abstracts, since 1952.

Writings in American History. New York: Grace Gardner Griffin, 1906 to 1940.

Newspaper Indexes of Current Events

Facts-on-File, since 1940; weekly.

New York Times Index, since 1913.

Wall Street Journal Index, monthly with annual cumulations.

Bibliography

Encyclopedias

The Americana Yearbook. New York: Grolier, since 1911.

The Book of the States. Chicago: Council of the State Governments, since 1935, biennial.

Encyclopedia of American Government. 3 vols. New York: Appleton-Century-Crofts, 1914.

Encyclopedia of Banking and Finance. Boston: Bankers, 1931.

Encyclopedia Brittanica. Chicago.

Encyclopedia of Educational Research. New York: Macmillan, 1950.

Encyclopedia of the Social Sciences. 15 vols. New York: Macmillan, 1930 to 1935.

Historical Statistics of the United States, 1789–1945. Washington, D.C.: Government Printing Office, 1949.

Municipal Yearbook. Chicago: International City Managers' Association, since 1934.

Social Security Yearbook. Washington, D.C.: Government Printing Office, since 1948.

Social Work Yearbook. New York: Russell Sage Foundation, since 1929.

Statesman's Yearbook. London: Macmillan, since 1864.

Statistical Abstract of the United States. Washington, D.C.: Bureau of the Census, since 1897.

Statistical Yearbook. New York: United Nations Statistical Office, since 1948.

World Almanac. New York, since 1869.

Bibliographical Dictionaries

The Biography Index. New York: H. W. Wilson, since 1946.

Who's Who. London: A. and C. Black, since 1849.

Who's Who in America. Chicago: Marquis, since 1899, biennial.

Who's Who in the Midwest. Chicago: Marquis, since 1949.

Bibliography

United States Government Documents

United States Government Publications, Catalogue. Washington, D.C.: Government Printing Office, since 1895.

State and Local Documents

Monthly Check List of State Publications. Washington, D.C.: Government Printing Office, since 1910.

Index